CW00433687

ABIDE

TEN WAYS TO DISCIPLE YOURSELF DEEPLY IN A WORLD THAT LOVES THE SHALLOW

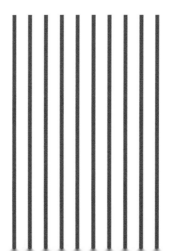

First published by Agonizo 2020

Copyright © 2020 by Joel Kaziro

Some Scriptures taken from The Message. Copyright © 1993, 1994, 1995, 1996, 2000, 2001, 2002. Used by permission of NavPress Publishing Group. Unless otherwise indicated, all Scripture quotations are taken from the Holy Bible, New International Version Anglicised Copyright © 1979, 1984, 2011 Biblica. Used by permission of Hodder & Stoughton Ltd, an Hachette UK company. All rights reserved.

All rights reserved. No part of this publication may be reproduced, stored or transmitted in any form or by any means, electronic, mechanical, photocopying, recording, scanning, or otherwise without written permission from the publisher. It is illegal to copy this book, post it to a website, or distribute it by any other means without permission.

Joel Kaziro has no responsibility for the persistence or accuracy of URLs for external or third-party Internet websites referred to in this publication and does not guarantee that any content on such Websites is, or will remain, accurate or appropriate.

First edition

If there's ever been a lesson I'd love to leave with my beloved Grace Church Youth, Heart Church Youth as well as the wonderful Heart Church YA, it's this one. Whilst our salvation is secure, abiding in Jesus is optional. You can either believe Him or believe the world, both are very good preachers.

JK

CONTENTS

PRAISE FOR ABIDE

"Abide is so honest, refreshing and easy to read that I can see many peoples lives being changed as they drink in the book."

Mark Ritchie
Evangelist, Edinburgh Fringe Festival Comedian

"This book is a great devotional/discipling experience, well suited for what I feel would be a younger audience. It seeks to not only engage people with the Bible, but more importantly its principles. It is straight talking and needs to be."

Malcolm Baxter
Senior Pastor, Heart Church Nottingham

"The best part of the book was how applicable it was to my own walk with Jesus. The questions at the end of each chapter helped me think through practical ways where I have either fallen into error or apathy. *Abide* is a fantastic book for believers of every age and experience. Read with an open heart and allow God to challenge you."

Luke Meadows
Founder, getdevoted.co.uk

"If read properly, *Abide* has the power to shape the way you live, the way you approach faith, your identity, and those around you. I implore you to spend time reflecting upon and critiquing this book."

Benjamin Etheridge
Former member of Heart Church Youth &
Durham University Student

FOREWORD

One of the big questions being asked of the global church at this present moment is not how do we get people to cross the thresholds of church or to tune into our online services, but rather how do we make mature disciples of Jesus.

With this book Joel arms the believer, the youth leader or the senior pastor with a much needed disciple-making tool. When read slowly and applied diligently will be a catalyst for lasting change, that matures people from decision to disciple, convert to Christian, responder to one who remains in him. Kaziro not only pens fundamental theological concepts full of truth but also gives the reader opportunity to embody abiding at appropriate intervals through the book.

This work flows from a genuine place of experience and empathy, it is more than a collection of thoughts, Joel Kaziro has remained in Christ for years and has been teaching others to do the same.

Abide is a continuation of what I have often listened to Joel speak to me about on long walks which seldom ended without Joel mentioning a book he was working on. May this be the first of many written works by Dr Joel Kaziro.

My prayer for this book is that those who read it would experience the fullness of joy that is the promised fruit of abiding in him and he in us. And that we would all (like Joel) become those who abide and teach others to do the same.

Thando Zulu
Hackney Church, London.
Former Youth Pastor at Heart Church, Nottingham

PREFACE

HOW TO READ THIS BOOK

Waking up with that familiar morning daze, you stop the alarm and do the usual morning scrolling. Just before the guilt sets in, you open up the good book. Three weeks late on your Bible reading plan, it's a discouraging Tuesday morning. The shower is pleasant, preparing you for the day ahead; it's going to be busy – it always is. Grabbing something quick, you set off with one prayer on your lips, 'Jesus, let me make it to five.'

Memories of Sunday drift by: hugs from the squad, the thank you from your mentor and the unmistakable presence of God. But it wasn't all good. The cliques were still cliques, the power politics were still bashing heads and everyone just seemed busy. You walk into work thinking the same thing we're all thinking – *I'm lost*. Not directionally, but scarier – lost in life.

> I know I'm a child of God, and I've done my Enneagram twenty times, but who am I? Of course Jesus loves me but who actually likes me? How does a ninety-minute service, some rushed prayer and giving to charity actually change the world?

If this reflects your own thoughts, take heart; you are not alone. There's no Alpha course for people like us, we've been to every seminar and listened to every podcast. We've been taught how to read our Bibles badly, are dissatisfied with our prayer lives and have reduced worship to singing. Yet we love our Bibles, want a more intimate prayer life and worship to touch every area of our lives. Likewise, we struggle with mental health, have way too many superficial friendships and find ourselves in the hurricane of culture wars from gender, to race, to politics and everything in between. We thought we'd found something. A theology. A tribe. A promotion. A mentor. A discipline. A party. A spouse. And when another pastor gets busted for embezzling money (James McDonald), abusive leadership (Mark Driscoll) or exploitation of church members (SPAC Nation), our world falls to pieces.

We are searching. And, whether you're a teen or 200, I'm convinced that we are *all* searching.

This is not any search.

It's *the* search.

The search for someone, not something. Someone that will do the wrestling for us. Someone that will, finally, let us breathe. If that's you, you've already met that person. This book is about staying in him. Stop searching; in Christ you've found what you've been looking for the whole time.

HOW TO USE THIS BOOK

Although it has five chapters, the book of 1 John is broken down into ten discipleship principles, which this book's ten chapters are based upon. While this is not a technical study of 1 John (for such an experience, please check out my editor Claire Musters' work on the letters of John), the apostle's letter is brilliant for understanding the goal of Christianity: to be with Christ. In other words, abiding. In this book, each chapter will follow this pattern: abiding in x, leads to y. Chapter one is about community. We'll look at why abiding in the light of Jesus' forgiveness allows you to take off your mask and find an authentic group of people that does the same. Chapter two is on the Bible. Taking the time to wrestle with Scripture leads to seeing God, your identity and the world around you much clearer. Chapter three is about rhythm. In a world that champions bigger, better and faster, it can be monumentally hard to develop sustainable routine. We will look at creating a personal pace of life that gives you room to work, grow and slow down. Chapter four is on discernment. We'll explore how knowing God's truth allows you to approach the bombardment of ads, worldviews and messages from culture we see every day with wisdom, learning the art of telling the truth from lies.

Chapter five is about the Father. While God is not engendered, as if he had testosterone, the title 'Father' is used by Jesus several times and holds particular meaning and significance. We'll unpack the idea of seeing God as Father and show how it leads us to an intimacy that eclipses anything we have on earth. Chapter six is about war. Once someone becomes a Christian, they take on an identity that puts them at odds with three enemies: the world (culture), the flesh (themselves) and the devil (Satan). Sin is more than wrongdoing; sin is allowing those three enemies to have victory in our lives, and so John shows us that abiding in Christ is the same as fighting those three enemies every day. Chapter seven calls us to harness the power of the Holy Spirit, which leads us to accomplish God's purposes with joyful obedience, rather than begrudging compliance.

The mountain peak of this book is chapter eight: love. The unfiltered, raw, ferociously huge and overwhelmingly heart-warming love of God is the glue that holds everything together. Chapter nine analyses why abiding in the love of God leads us to freedom – a freedom that allows us to love ourselves, our friends and even our enemies. Finally, chapter ten serves as the epilogue with one simple statement: there's more. Abiding in Jesus has convinced me that you were made for more: more courage, more love, more meaning and, ultimately, more life.

****

This book is not long. You could read it in four hours but, if you just did that, you'd miss the entire point. At the end of each chapter is a section called 'Stop & Think', where I provide some probing questions about poignant topics such as life, death, identity, purpose, fear etc. So please read prayerfully, critically and reflectively.

While you won't agree with everything in this book, in order to get the best from it, you're going to have to take some time to digest it. Talk to God, meditate, toss around your thoughts, feelings and reactions like a juggling ball.

> Jesus, what does this mean for me? What does this show me about You? How will this affect my day to day?

Let your prayer be a minute-by-minute, day-by-day back and forth between you and God. Prayer does not always need to be focused and heavy, but frequent and varied. While you're walking, working, photocopying, sending emails and working out, allow yourself to have a constant conversation with God. If abide means to live within something, see this book as living within prayer.

What does it mean to read critically? We live in a world that's so trigger-ready, scouring social media for the first sign of something we like, or something we hate, in order to pledge our allegiance or hostility to anyone we agree or disagree with respectively – unloading a barrage of comments, emojis, likes and dislikes. The social media algorithm is created to value and highlight extremist views, which makes the majority think they have far less in common with others than they actually do[1].

> He said he was pro-life – hit like. She said she isn't a feminist – let me give her a piece of my mind. They're liberal – retweet, share and comment, telling the racist, *Daily Mail*-loving, homophobic, BNP/UKIP/ Brexit-voting conservatives where to stick it. They're conservative – retweet, share and comment, crushing those fluffy, *Guardian*-reading, too-woke-to-function,

Bible-hating, bleeding-heart liberals.

Please, please, please, don't be a stereotypical 'tolerant' millennial, dismissing my worldview and ranting about it on social media – engage the text. Wrestle with it. Critique it. Our generation has sadly lost the art of discussion, preferring to just shut down a conversation at the first sign of offense. To read critically means to read everything before reacting, thinking through what is helpful and what is unhelpful.

Lastly, we come to reading reflectively. The great reformer Martin Luther said, 'Our Lord and Master Jesus Christ willed the entire life of believers to be one of repentance[2].' Most Christians think of repentance as a cross between S&M and a prayer meeting: whipping ourselves because of our guilty conscience. No grace and no joy, just a bruised back. While we should have remorse over our sin, the more important question is *why* don't we follow God's commands? In the Bible, the Greek word for repentance is *metanoeite*: 'meta', which means change, and 'noieo', which means think. The best translation for this word would be 'change your thinking'.

> God said don't steal, but if I don't have those trainers, the
> guys are going to rip me to pieces.

This was one of my journal entries as I was struggling with envy. I didn't know why I kept falling into almost overwhelming feelings of jealousy with my boys. What helped me? God changed my thinking. Jesus was the perfect man. An impoverished, single, Palestinian rabbi, who happened to be God in the flesh. He never ran for political office, won a war or owned any property. He struggled to pay his taxes, hung out with paupers and priests, and was executed like a common criminal. Why then, did Jesus never get insecure about his status?

> Look at the birds of the air; they do not sow or reap

or store away in barns, and yet your heavenly Father feeds them. Are you not much more valuable than they? (Matthew 6:26).

Thinking about Jesus' words changes it all. I want status. I want approval. I want people to see my stuff and think I'm a G³. However, Jesus tells me that God already sees me as precious. Therefore, why do I care so much about what others think? Repentance isn't feeling guilty over envy, it's striving to believe that God's is the only opinion that counts.

God doesn't want you to give up the way you live and drag you kicking and screaming into a regressive religion. God wants to lead you into the most fulfilled life you could ever have. So think of repentance as a moment when the penny drops; after living one way, which you thought was the best way, God's way suddenly comes to life and seems like a much better way to do it. And so you do it gladly, rather than with resentment. Therefore, having read, prayed, critiqued and found the gold at the bottom of the mine, your final step is to actually live a different way. Here's a quick recap:

1. Read: Read the relevant portion of 1 John and a chapter of this book.
2. Pray: Use the questions to talk to God throughout your day.
3. Critique: Take what's helpful from the chapter and drop what isn't.
4. Reflect: Think about how this will change your day-to-day life.

Ten chapters and one fantastic apostle's letter. Are you ready for this adventure? Let's dive in.

COMMUNITY

ABIDE IN AUTHENTICITY

1

This is the message we have heard from him and proclaim to you, that God is light, and in him is no darkness at all.

If we say we have fellowship with him while we walk in darkness, we lie and do not practice the truth. But if we walk in the light, as he is in the light, we have fellowship with one another, and the blood of Jesus his Son cleanses us from all sin.

If we say we have no sin, we deceive ourselves, and the truth is not in us. If we confess our sins, he is faithful and just to forgive us our sins and to cleanse us from all unrighteousness. If we say we have not sinned, we make him a liar, and his word is not in us.

1 John 1:5 - 10

Imagine being born blind. You stumble in the darkness, feeling your way through life using your other senses. It is impossible to fully comprehend a sunrise or the grandeur of a mountain landscape through others' descriptions of them. Now imagine everyone was the same as you. No one had ever seen anything. The sunrise wasn't beautiful; it was just warm. Glaciers weren't captivating; they were just cold. Niagara Falls would just be wet, the Grand Canyon would just be breezy, and we wouldn't even know that stars exist. Now imagine that you gave your working eyes to just one of these poor folks. How elated, confused and excited would they be?! Moreover, how odd would they start to sound to everybody else? How do you describe colour to someone who has never seen?

Humankind is spiritually blind. We stumble in the darkness unaware of the glory, beauty and majesty of God. However Jesus, the light of the world, opened the eyes of John and, in the opening paragraph of his letter, John cannot help but shout about the cure that brought light into his darkness. He's touched it, seen it and felt it. He will not be happy until everyone shares in his joy! People who love something can't stop shouting about it. That is the two-pronged nature of being human: devotion and evangelism[4]. Take kids who love ice cream. They eat it, study all the different flavours and become overnight connoisseurs. When that familiar jingle is heard in the distance, parents and siblings everywhere get their earplugs and riot shields ready for the imminent 'Ice cream van!' followed by the customary stampede.

Too childish? Let's take another example. Take someone that's just started a good relationship. Before long, their partner becomes a routine feature in their everyday language: 'Jake loves chicken too!', 'I don't know if Kwame and I can make it tonight' or 'I need to call Anish first'. In fact, once people are settled in a good relationship, they can start feeling sorry for single people. Before meeting Clare, I was single for about a decade. I can't tell you the amount of times my married friends turned to me, looked deeply into my eyes, laid a hand on my shoulder and said, 'Joel, we need to get you a wife'. The reason I was always surprised by this comment was not because I was single, but because the topic of conversation had had nothing to do with relationships up until that point. They bred it into every conversation. Their devotion lead to their evangelism.

THE DEVOTED SAMARITAN EVANGELIST

In John's most famous book, the gospel of John, is a well-known story about Jewish man, meeting a Samaritan woman. This is my retelling of this encounter, with some artistic licence. The original can be found in John 4:1–30. This is what it means for devotion to lead to evangelism.

****

A Jewish man approached a lone Samaritan woman. She was stunning, yet timid. She was drawing water at a well in the scorch of the midday sun. The morning crowd had kicked her out for being...her. The Jewish man politely asked the lady for a drink, which wasn't appropriate as Jewish-Samaritan relations were about as friendly as white-black relations in 1960s America. She was alarmed at his request. Not only was he a Jew, but he had no cup and Jacob's well was deep.

The Samaritan woman had been in several marriages, each relationship brimming with affection at first but, after a while, terminating in heartbreak and disgrace. After the fifth, she promised herself never again; she presented her body but withdrew her heart. She didn't have any formal education and so she figured her breasts would pay her rent – and it worked. That life led to isolation. She was often ridiculed by her religious kinsmen, desperate to pick up some rubble and end her struggle. The sun was severe, but the alternative was unbearable; such is life for a sinner. Life as an outcast was more tolerable than living every day in fear. As they talked, she realized that he knew.

'The fact is, you have had five husbands, and the man you now have is not your husband' (v.17). People usually had bits and pieces of her story, but he'd seen every skeleton in her closet. Her eyes darted for an escape. Nothing. Just him, her and the well. If she screamed, no one would hear. If she ran, he would catch her. He had the callouses of a carpenter; it wouldn't take much.

Trying to hide her tremor, she replied: 'Sir, I can see that you are a prophet. Our ancestors worshipped on this mountain, but you Jews claim that the place where we must worship is in Jerusalem' (v.20).

He moved closer. 'Woman, believe me, a time is coming when you will worship the Father neither on this mountain nor in Jerusalem. You Samaritans worship what you do not know; we worship what we do know, for salvation is from the Jews' (vv.21–22). His voice was soft, his glance was piercing. The gap grew smaller.

'I know that Messiah is coming. When he comes, he will explain everything to us' (v.25). Like all Samaritans, she believed that, one day, a Messiah would end all her hardship. The anointed one would bring justice and hope to the downtrodden. She closed her eyes…and stopped resisting. If this was it, this was it.

He reached out and clasped her hand. 'I, the one speaking to you – I am he' (v.26). His whisper melted something cold. A man was speaking to her without his mind wandering to immoral places. Instead of the usual overtones of violence, a man was speaking to her, a defiled woman, with love. After decades of closing off her heart from a hostile world, this man brought it to life again.

In her euphoria, she dropped her jar and ran. She raced back to the same streets on which she used to flee from society, telling as many people who would listen that the Messiah had come, and his name was Jesus.

* * *

Her devotion led to her evangelism. That's what humans do, regardless of their religion. This devoted Samaritan evangelist's story is our story. Abiding in the light means resting in the knowledge that after being blind for so long, Jesus has given us sight. Christians should not be people that pray, go to church nor meet with God because they must. Rather, we meet with God because it's our privilege. The more we know and love God, the more he will become an everyday part of our language. Of course, it's difficult to share your faith in a secular society, but, then again, it's always been difficult to describe colour to the blind.

Although we love God, we do, say and think things that are heinous to him. When we attempt to live God's way, our hearts are never 100 per cent holy, our actions are never 100 per cent altruistic and our minds are never 100 per cent pure. The Bible calls this sin – both a failure to meet God's standards when we try and a rebellion against God's commands when we disobey. So, what do we do? We are both rebels and failures…and God is the Almighty judge.

Jesus' death on the cross means that we can come to God and lay our sin, shame and guilt at his feet. All has been forgiven in Christ. We certainly do not run *from* God, scared that he is going to harm us. Instead we run *to* God who allowed his Son to be harmed because of our failures. He does not condemn me; rather the forgiveness of God empowers me to live a more upright life. Therein is the cycle of sanctification (see Hebrews 10:11–18; 1 Peter 2:1–3). We sin, we repent, he forgives and we grow. We sin, we repent, he forgives and we grow. We are no longer condemned sinners but saints that stumble.

STOP & THINK

Abiding in Jesus means abiding in his light. We, by nature, are creatures of darkness (Ephesians 5:8–14). By bringing our darkness into the light, Jesus eradicates the darkness within us. The wonderful thing about abiding in Christ is that we are all in this together. Not only do we all sin, but we all have a Saviour to whom we can take our filth. We need not wear a mask. We need not hide our struggles. We can be a people marked by a regular confession of sins to one another (James 5:16). Why hide? All have been forgiven in Christ. So here are the questions we need to answer:

One: Do you think that you are a sinner?

This may sound obvious, but one of the largest misconceptions about the word sin is that it refers to those who commit rape, murder or paedophilia. It's so abhorrent that it can only be used for the true degenerates of our society. Most people would believe they are good – not perfect, but reasonably decent and upright. But that definition of sin does not go anywhere near far enough. Sin absolutely describes the horrendous crimes aforementioned, but sin also describes any thought, word or action that goes against God's commandments. The time you lied to your parents. That's sin. The time you thought the girl or guy across the room would look great naked. That's sin. The time you thought you were a 'better' Christian, Man U fan or father than your friend who struggles with prayer, can't make every game and forgets his kids' birthdays. That's sin. The minor offences we make, as well as the major ones, are all detestable in the eyes of God. So what do you think now? Are you a sinner?

Two: Do you see the depth of your sin?

If you were the only person to have ever sinned on planet earth, Jesus would still have come down from heaven to be nailed to that cross in order to pay the cosmic penalty for your crimes against God. So how do you feel about your sin now?

Three: Do you confess your sin?

Confession is an art largely lost in the Protestant world, yet it is still a significant part of Catholic and Orthodox practice. Confession is the act of naming your sin and sorrowfully bringing it to God. Although we will never be able to name all the sins we ever commit, confession shows our remorse and our intention to return to God. This should happen with God first but should also involve community. In other words, your closest friends and family should know where you fall and vice-versa – for the Bible says that we should 'Carry each other's burdens' (Galatians 6:2). The alternative is that no one knows what sins you struggle with and you end up wearing a mask of pretence, fearful that people might find out about the real and flawed side of you.

Four: Do you repent?

This entire chapter is about dealing with the fact that we think and do terrible things in the eyes of God, but that God has not only forgiven our filth but empowers us to overcome and stop doing these things. As we discussed in the preface, repentance (*metanoeite* in Greek) means to change your thinking. Therefore, do you practice repentance? Do you let God change the way you think?

Five: Do you realize that you are a saint?

All this talk of sin may sound condemning. Sin this. Sin that. It's forgiven but it's inescapable. Nonsense. In Christ, *all* your sin has been forgiven. In Christ, we are no longer sinners, but saints (1 Corinthians 1:2). Like a white dress that can no longer be stained, you have been, are being and will be washed in the cleansing blood of Christ. The cross means that you are, and forever will remain, white as snow. Therefore, no longer should you refer to yourself as a sinner that may do saintly things, but a saint that is tripped up by sin. This isn't because of anything you have done, but the free grace of God.

Six: Have you crafted your community?

This chapter calls you to life in community. Jesus' sacrifice has set you free, forgiven every minor and major blemish that you have ever done, and now he calls Christians everywhere to follow in his footsteps as the clean and pure children of God. However, walking this path is not easy, and walking in the light literally means that we put our mess on show. This was, and still is, one of the hardest aspects of the Christian faith – authentic community. In this modern, ultra-connected world, we can easily find community: social media, sports teams, hobbies, hangouts, quidditch appreciation societies and the list goes on. However, what is in short supply is *authentic* community. People who know the real you.

The hard thing about walking in the light is that Jesus doesn't just clean you up and then your problems automatically cease. Walking in the light exposes you – both the beauty and the beast within. Therefore, if you're going to follow Jesus successfully, you're going to need help. People who know the real you. They need to both call you on your mess and push you to greatness.

Theologians group Jesus' disciples in terms of proximity (see figure 1). There were the multitudes of followers that he would teach extensively but spend little time with. Then there were the seventy-two whom he personally gave teaching, training and assignment to. Next came an even smaller division, the twelve disciples. This group was Jesus' entourage; wherever Jesus was, there they were, often doing ministry together as well as sharing meals, recreation and rest times together.

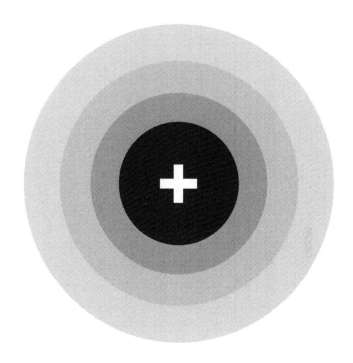

━━━ **THE INNER CIRCLE: PETER, JAMES & JOHN**

━━━ THE TWELVE DISCIPLES

━━━ THE SEVENTY-TWO FOLLOWERS

━━━ THE THOUSANDS OF THE MULTITUDE

FIGURE 1: JESUS' COMMUNITY IN
CONCENTRIC CIRCLES

However, Jesus had an even smaller group of men that seemed to be his closest friends. To Peter, James and John, he gave special insight: they witnessed his transfiguration, the temptation at the garden of Gethsemane and he even introduced them to Moses and Elijah!

Clare is the middle of my world. We spend almost every evening together, do ministry together, share finances, know each other's families well – and also know one another's deepest and darkest secrets. Ours is the closest human relationship I've ever had, which is why I decided to marry her. Outside Clare, I have four people in my life who have walked alongside me for almost a decade: Jon, Hannah, Helen and Beth. I'm closest to Jon and have great relationships with the others. Jon and I have walked through break-ups, promotions, babies, marriages, faith breakthroughs and faith breakings, suffering and even death. Outside Clare, those four people are the first to know where and how I come off the rails and have full permission to speak frankly into my life. When the inner circle works, it works wonders because it reveals all my failures. Together, these five speak life and hope into my mess and have helped me grow into the man I am today.

I, however, am a black man.

While guys tend to walk through life alone, in my experience, the majority of black men have turned this into a sport. The hardest thing about the inner circle is the difficult conversation that can be directed at my shortcomings. Those times when they disapprove of my over-working lifestyle and the confrontations about my inappropriate and hurtful jokes (even if they are comedic gold). Community is easy. Authentic community is hard, because it allows someone else to have authority in your life. Why use the word authentic? Because when it's done properly, it's messy. I can't tell you the number of arguments, fallouts and misunderstandings I've had with these five. But, what do you get in return?

Intimacy.

When you first went to Jesus, he looked at all your mess and decided to both forgive it as well as help you overcome it. Walking in the light means allowing other people to do the very same thing. The intimacy of a good friendship will improve your mental health, hold you stable in times of unrest and finally put to rest this seemingly insatiable quest towards finding a lover. Jesus was the most fulfilled being who ever lived, and yet he was single. Paul was the most effective missionary in the history of the church and, again, he was single. Surely their lives and their legacies are enough to convince a marriage-idolising Western church that true intimacy is not found exclusively in a romantic relationship, but rather is an essential component of a true relationship, whether it be romantic or platonic.

With all this in mind, I urge you: craft your community. Find a group of friends with whom you can be vulnerable, sharing your ups, downs, sins, dreams, failures and aspirations. People that know you. People with whom you can take off the mask without fear of judgement or rejection. People that challenge you, but make you feel safe. People that you can veg out with, as well as shoot for the stars. Find your team. Find your squad. Without it, you are missing out on the genuine pleasures of life that God has called us all to.

BIBLE

ABIDE IN THE WORD

2

I am writing to you, little children, because your sins are forgiven for his name's sake.

I am writing to you, fathers, because you know him who is from the beginning.

I am writing to you, young men, because you have overcome the evil one.

I write to you, children, because you know the Father.

I write to you, fathers, because you know him who is from the beginning.

I write to you, young men, because you are strong, and the word of God abides in you, and you have overcome the evil one.

1 John 2:12 - 14

How well do you know your Bible? Have a go at this quiz. The answers can be found in Appendix One:

1. Who wrote the first five books of the Old Testament?
2. Why did God rescue his people from slavery under Pharaoh in Egypt?
3. Who was king of Israel before David?
4. If the Northern Kingdom was called Israel, what was the Southern Kingdom called?
5. Why did God send prophets to his people in the Old Testament?
6. Who told everyone that Jesus was coming?
7. What did Jesus tell all Christians to do before ascending to heaven?
8. What happened when Peter the Apostle preached for the first time in Jerusalem?
9. What was Paul / Saul of Tarsus doing before he became a Christian?
10. What book of the Bible describes the end of the world?

BIBLICAL ILLITERACY

I'm thirty-two. I've never enrolled in any formal theological education and have been a Christian for about eighteen years. The reason I tell you this is that I'm startled at the number of people that have been Christians far longer than I yet marvel at my knowledge of the Bible. The problem is, I genuinely don't know it that well! I think most Christians view their Bible as we viewed our greens as infants. While our mothers repeatedly told us that peas were good for us, chips tasted better. At worst, we'd throw a tantrum and at best, we'd swallow them reluctantly. At no point would a seven-year-old enjoy eating their greens. We find ourselves in a situation where most Christians know they should not only read their Bible but should also love it. However, so many of us struggle to do either. A large study on Bible reading in America was conducted by the Barna Group in 2014[5] and the results were startling:

- Seventy-nine per cent of Americans consider the Bible to be sacred.
- Eighty-eight per cent own a Bible, with an average of three Bibles per household.
- Sixty-nine per cent of practising Christians can name the first five books of the Bible.
- Fifty-two per cent believe the Bible discourages pornography.
- Forty-five per cent read the Bible at least once a month or more.
- Forty-seven per cent of adults believe that they never have enough time to read it.
- Twenty-two per cent believe that it's difficult to understand, interpret and have trouble finding the stories or verses they are looking for.

Let's go back to the quiz. How did you do? I would say it was a moderately easy quiz. If you did well, don't get too happy, as you're in the minority. If you did badly, don't get too discouraged, as there are many people in the same boat as you. I didn't throw this quiz in to shame or exalt you, but rather to show you the problem: biblical illiteracy.

The results from the Barna Group's survey reveal a problem. We love the Bible and believe it to be the inspired Word of God, but don't take the time to study it. Then, bursting with inspiration on the way back from a conference, we decide to have another go. We crack it open and the language does not make sense, the books are in a weird order and our brains are overwhelmed with the genealogies, commands, prophets and weird talking donkeys. By day five, we're back to mornings with

Hillsong and the verse of the day...again. What's the result? Well, we start to believe things that are contrary to the story of the Bible – like the other forty-eight percent in the survey that believe it condones pornography.

THE WHAT, THE HOW & THE WHY

So, what's the solution to our Bible illiteracy problem? We need to change our perspective of the Bible and start to devour it like Ben and Jerry's Phish Food on a warm summer afternoon. The problem with our relationship to the Bible is that we do not understand what it is, how to read it and what difference it should make in our lives. In essence, we don't know the what, the how or the why. This chapter seeks to provide a basic understanding of those three principles and allow you to begin a rich and fulfilling journey into the word of God.

Start with Jesus

Billions sing his praises every week. Others dedicate their lives to critiquing his work. Some kill in his name. Others are killed because of his name. The foundation of the most popular religion ever. The most significant figure in world history. The life on which time is divided into BC and AD. The cornerstone of the Christian faith. The only man, they say, to have beaten death.

Jesus of Nazareth.

The word Christian means 'little Christ', yet its startling how many Christians know so little about Christ himself. No Harry Potter fan has ever complained of reading too much Harry Potter. Although I'm not a fan of witches and wizards myself, I'm always startled at how devoted fans were to the series. When a new book came out, they were more than happy to camp outside Waterstones all night for a chance to delve into the world of Hogwarts and try their hand at 'Expelliarmus'.

The point of this chapter is to encourage you to start a reading plan that will deepen your knowledge of Jesus. Dissect him. Analyze him. Put him underneath the microscope. Why did people think he was a fraud? Why was he the Son of God? Go and create a more solid biblical foundation for your faith.

At times you will be perplexed, angered by his words or warmed by his love. Follow him through cities and slums. Listen to his lectures. Laugh at his jokes. Cry at his betrayal and witness his execution. Meet his family, greet his friends and encounter his enemies. Herein is the wonder of the Bible.

Remember, you're not reading fiction. Jesus actually walked the earth, was literally executed and did it all for you. He even got a few mates to write the whole thing down meticulously, so you would have a reminder of how much he endured in order for you to enjoy him forever. He is the point behind it all and the rock on which we build our faith.

Where can we find out the truth about Jesus? The Bible and ancient history. The New Testament contains four accounts on the life of Jesus: the gospels of Matthew, Mark, Luke and John. Since the gospels were written to distinct types of people, they were all written in different ways:

- Mark's gospel was written first. It was for Romans who wanted to know the facts – who, what, when, where. It's the earliest, shortest and easiest gospel to read.
- Luke's gospel is like Mark expanded. It was written for one of Luke's apprentices called Theophilus. Since Luke was a doctor, his inner geek came out as he wrote about Jesus with more detail and depth.

- Matthew's gospel was for Jews. Since converting to Christianity may have meant leaving their communities, Jews needed to know that Jesus was the Messiah promised in the Old Testament. His gospel looks at Jesus' teaching the most.
- If the first three gospels are rock, pop and hip-hop, John's gospel is jazz. It uses symbolism and abstract concepts to communicate the true depths of Jesus' identity. John's gospel was written last and focuses more on the divinity of Jesus. The first three gospels focus on Jesus' life: what, when and where. John focuses on Jesus' identity (see figure 2).

The Jesus Plan

Start your Bible reading by focusing on learning more about Jesus (see appendix two). Pick a gospel and read it. If you're completely new to this, pick Mark. Read a chapter a day. At the end of each chapter, stop and think about these four questions:

1. Where was Jesus?
2. What was Jesus doing?
3. Why was he doing this?
4. Who did Jesus think he was?

Jesus' locations were particularly important. For example, as a man raised in the Jewish region of Galilee, why did he travel to non-Jewish regions? (Mark 7:24). Was he on holiday? Business? Running from the authorities? Jesus' activities were also important. Sometimes he would attack public property (Mark 11:15), heal the critically ill (Mark 5:35–43) or teach thousands of followers (Mark 10:1).

However, knowing Jesus' whereabouts and actions aren't enough. There are reasons why Jesus did what he did, and those reasons span out of who Jesus knew he was and the purpose he was on earth for. This is the crux of our study: deepening your knowledge of Jesus. His thoughts. His actions. His impact on the world. Some say he taught, performed miracles and served his country because he was a faithful Jewish rabbi (Jewish teacher). His followers called him the Son of God. His enemies said he was a false prophet and had him killed. The point is to treat Jesus as a real person.

Welcome to an adventure into the life of Jesus Christ, where we explore the where, what, why and who of the most controversial Jewish teachers who has ever existed.

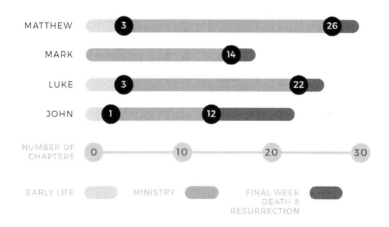

BREAKING DOWN THE GOSPELS
The Three Parts of Jesus' Story

FIGURE 2: THE THREE PARTS OF
JESUS LIFE IN EACH GOSPEL

WHAT IS THE BIBLE?

The Jewish sacred book is called the Tanakh (or the Miqra). Written mostly in Hebrew with a bit of Aramaic, the Tanakh consists of thirty-nine books that you and I call the Old Testament:

- Torah (5 books) aka 'The Law'
- Nevi'im (21 books) aka 'The Prophets'
- Ketuvim (13 books) aka 'The Writings'.

Jesus was a rabbi from Nazareth – a small and poor town in Palestine. He called twelve men to be his devoted students and used the Tanakh to teach them how to follow God. As we shall see, he was executed for saying the Tanakh was about him (blasphemy) and his followers started calling him their saviour ie The 'Christ'.

During the first century, assemblies of these 'Christ-worshippers' started to meet in cities all around Mediterranean Sea. 'Christianity' spread like wildfire and soon, Jews and non-Jews were starting to worship Jesus. What's another word for assembly?

Church.

Some of the twelve began to write to their various churches to encourage them, correct any wayward beliefs or give them a telling off for unhelpful behaviour. They produced two types of documents: epistles and gospels. Epistles are letters written to specific churches or groups of people. Gospels are accounts about the life, death and resurrection of Jesus.

These weren't trivial notes. The new churches viewed these documents as their highest authority since they were written by Jesus' closest friends. Many people today have heard of such documents: the gospel of John, the letter to the Corinthians, etc. Sound familiar? These are the twenty-seven books we call the 'New Testament'.

But what about the Tanakh?

These 'Christians' also loved the Tanakh since it pointed to Jesus. Therefore, it was necessary to compile all these writings into one book. After several meetings over hundreds of years, the church published the official list of books that all Christians called 'holy' at the start of the 5th century. They called it the 'canon'. We call it the Bible. It includes:

Thirty-nine Jewish books from the Tanakh.

One gospel from Levi (aka Matthew).

One gospel from Mark.

One gospel and Acts from Luke.

One gospel, three epistles and a vision from John.

Thirteen epistles from Paul.

Two epistles from Peter.

One epistle from Jesus' brother James.

One epistle from Jesus' brother Jude.

Who is the central figure of all these writings? God. Every word of the Bible is written to lead you to the feet of the one who put stars in space and hair on your head. He is the Creator, sustainer, merciful, wrathful, Almighty, sovereign and the main character of our divine drama.

Sixty-six books.

Three languages.

Two Testaments.

One story.

THE JEWISH CHURCH

Following his resurrection, Jesus left his twelve disciples with a mission to spread the Good News about him all over the world.

Since Jesus' followers were in the Jewish capital of Jerusalem, Christianity started as a faith consisting of Jews. Then God inspired the believers at a festival known as Pentecost (see Acts 2). Filled with boldness, they did as Jesus commanded and taught in many synagogues that Jesus was the promised Messiah (or 'Christ') that rose from the dead. The original twelve disciples were the leading patriarchs of the movement and came to be known as the Apostles. Peter became the head of the church and worked alongside John to govern this embryonic society. 'They [the early church] devoted themselves to the apostles' teaching and the fellowship, to the breaking of bread and to prayer' (Acts 2:42).

The 'Jewish' church was quite a remarkable sight; it broke all socio-economic divisions. The rich shared their wealth with the poor. The diseased ate alongside the healthy. They faced fierce persecution yet miracles of healing and deliverance followed them everywhere as the lame walked and the blind saw.

One of the clearest markers of Christian faith was fierce commitment to community: they ate together, prayed together, suffered together and, in many cases, died together.

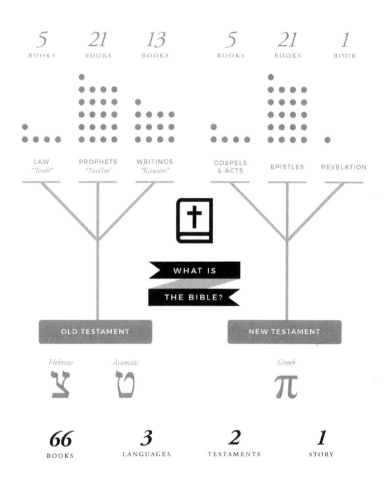

FIGURE 3: WHAT IS THE BIBLE?

With Peter as the leader, James, Jude and the author of Hebrews (currently unknown) are letters that were written to predominantly Jewish communities. Their numbers swelled as thousands of Jewish families were added day by day to this new community of faith (Acts 2:41). They were such a counter-cultural people that they started to be referred to as 'The Way' (Acts 9:2).

As more Jews believed their message, the Scribes and Pharisees (Jewish rulers) were both astonished and angry that this movement had not been crushed. Annas and Caiaphas (the chief rulers) were the two main Jewish opponents of the church, arresting, beating and punishing the apostles wherever possible. Unable to disrupt such a movement, they called on a bigger gun – Saul of Tarsus.

Saul was one of the most devout Jews in 1st-century Jerusalem. Discipled by the great Gamaliel, Saul spoke at least three languages and had memorized the Scriptures. Offended at the church's blasphemy, Saul took it as his personal mission to destroy the Jewish believers. He would go from door to door, dragging believers from their homes, throwing them into prison, beating them in public or, worse still, executing them. He didn't work alone but trained others to do the same. Young, sharp and driven, Saul became the first religious terrorist to strike fear into the early church, scattering them throughout Judea and Samaria.

Then Saul met Jesus.

On a routine trip to Damascus to harass more church folk, Saul had a powerful vision of Jesus (Acts 9). Everything he believed about 'The Way' changed on that road. From persecutor to promoter, Saul (who was also known as Paul) conversion was especially important. With Paul on the team, the Jewish church was about to undergo something that would change its identity forever: realizing that Jesus had come for everyone, not just them. You can read about the Jewish church in the first nine chapters of Acts and the letters that were written specifically to Jewish audiences: James, Jude, 1 Peter, 2 Peter and Hebrews. Appendix 2B is a reading plan to help you understand the Jewish early church. As you read, stop and think about these four questions:

1. What was the Holy Spirit doing?
2. What were the disciples doing?
3. Who loved the church? Why?
4. Who hated the church? Why?

THE TRANSITION OF THE CHURCH

By the time we get to Acts 10, the church is spreading – but it is still Jewish. They worship in synagogues, observe Jewish law and worship Jesus as the Messiah. But Jesus instructed the disciples to spread the Gospel to Judea (locally), Samaria (nationally) and the ends of the earth (internationally) (see Acts 1:8). He never intended it to be exclusively Jewish, yet it was still Jewish custom not to mix with Gentiles (non-Jews). Strict Jews weren't even allowed to eat with them. In Acts 10, Cornelius was the first Gentile to receive the Holy Spirit. Peter, led by a vision to his home, went and baptized him into the faith. Cornelius' conversion began the transition of the church from Jewish to universal.

The debate about whether Gentiles could be accepted into the church raged on as Paul and Barnabas spread the gospel to towns in south-central Turkey amongst the region of Galatia. As Gentiles became Christians, Paul wrote the book of Galatians, where he controversially said:

> We Jews know that we have no advantage of birth over 'non-Jewish sinners'. We know very well that we are not set right with God by rule-keeping but only through personal faith in Jesus Christ. How do we know? We

tried it—and we had the best system of rules the world has ever seen! Convinced that no human being can please God by self-improvement, we believed in Jesus as the Messiah so that we might be set right before God by trusting in the Messiah, not by trying to be good (Galatians 2:15–16, *The Message*).

The church had some incredibly difficult questions to ponder and significant decisions to make. If someone believed in Jesus as the Messiah, did they still have to observe Torah (Jewish law)? If not, then what? Should they throw out their rituals and religious practice completely? Could Jesus-loving Jews eat bacon? As more Jews believed in Jesus, those that didn't convert grew more outraged. King Herod Agrippa, grandson of the same Herod who massacred babies to try and kill Jesus (Matthew 2:16–18), ordered James to be beheaded and put Peter in prison. God had other plans as an angel broke him out and killed the monarch (Acts 12).

Amid the expansion, the controversy and the persecution of the early church, the transitionary period came to a climax as all the church leaders met in Jerusalem for the first official churchwide conference in Acts 15. It was there that they decided that Christians did not have to observe the religious Jewish law.

You can read about the transition of the church in Acts 10–15 as well as the book of Galatians. Appendix 2C shows the church in transition reading plan and a basic map of Paul and Barnabas' missionary trip. As you read, stop and think about these four questions:

1. What was the Holy Spirit doing?
2. What were the disciples doing?
3. Where was the Gospel going?
4. Who hated the church? Why?

THE UNIVERSAL CHURCH

The remainder of Acts is dedicated to the twelve apostles venturing into the known world, spreading the Christian faith in large cities and starting churches all around the Mediterranean basin. Paul was the most prolific of these Apostles, embarking on two more missionary journeys to south-eastern Greece and west Turkey. Different churches were born in different cultures and, as they began to live as Christians in different contexts, problems arise that Paul (and his partners) addressed through writing letters to them.

Timothy and Titus were Paul's church-planting apprentices in Ephesus and Crete respectively. In the books of Timothy and Titus, Paul wrote to them to explain how to build, care and appoint leaders for a church. These are referred to as the 'pastoral' epistles and are very useful if you want to know how to become a godly leader.

Paul wasn't the only letter writer. Jude was Jesus' brother and, having finally put his faith in God, became a weapon that God used mightily to protect his church. And so, Jude boldly wrote to a church under attack. Another writer, John, helped Timothy at the church in Ephesus before he was banished to the isle of Patmos.

By Acts 23, Paul was prompted by the Holy Spirit to go to Jerusalem and preach that Jesus was the Messiah who had been promised in the Old Testament. He caused such an uproar that the Romans arrested him to keep the peace. Although Paul was Jewish, he was a Roman citizen, and so eventually stood trial in Rome.

The church started sending missionaries all over the world: Andrew and Philip ventured north to Turkey and Eastern Europe; Simon went south to northern Africa; Thomas and Bartholomew sailed east to India; Paul travelled west to Greece, Italy and Spain.

For the first time in history, anyone could be part of God's people – the universal church was born. Go and read about it using appendix 2D: The Universal Church Reading Plan.

It's important to recognize that the New Testament started with a murdered Jewish rabbi, but the same Spirit that rose Jesus from the dead started a movement. That movement made Peter the fisherman into Peter the leader. Peter converted Stephen, who converted Saul. Saul became Paul. In AD 312, Caesar declared Christianity the state religion of Rome. Rome converted Britain and, ultimately, converted us. And now it's our turn.

Look around you to see that the church is still growing. Look within to understand that you continue to carry a message that sets the world on fire. Look up, as God is still on the move and his Gospel is not finished.

I know that so far I haven't provided a reading plan for the Old Testament and the book of Revelation, but starting with Jesus and the early church is a great way to grow in a robust understanding of the Bible. Start with Jesus, move onto the Jewish Church, navigate the transition and finish with the universal church. Use the reading plans to guide your study and, once you incorporate it into a rhythm, it will unlock your understanding of God's Word. Now we know *what* we have to read, and in a helpful order. The second question is: *how* do we read the Bible?

HOW TO READ THE BIBLE

Hermeneutics, the four-syllable terror-of-a-word, simply means 'the art of interpreting the Bible'. If you're going to abide in the Word, it's essential to learn hermeneutics. Easy, right? Although it's a fancy word, hermeneutics is better explained by the acronym SOAP: Scripture, Observation, Application and Prayer. This is often the way Bible study is taught in Sunday School, but it's often taught badly and all too quickly. So, here I give you ten tips to abide in the Word, which is basically SOAP explained.

SCRIPTURE

One: Make a plan

The first question is essential: what are you going to read? My suggestion would be to start with the gospels. Fall in love with Jesus. From there move on to the foundations of the early church in Acts. As we've already said, these letters get into all the problems Paul and Peter had with all the churches they established all over Europe and the Middle East. The Corinthians loved sex and getting drunk in church. The Galatians preferred religion to the Gospel. The Thessalonians were getting upset because their members kept getting killed and the Philippians were the annoyingly perfect church that you or I wouldn't have got into. Make a plan that's fun. I usually read about a chapter a day, but have had times when I've done a verse a day. Make a plan that you can stick to easily. Make a plan that's yours. (If you prefer to follow a reading plan, try using the ones I've already flagged up to you – found in the appendices).

Two: Decide where and when

It's imperative that you set aside regular time to intentionally study God's Word. Remember, you want to make this a lifestyle, not a seasonal burst. This is eating and drinking, not training for a marathon: one you do all the time; the other you do for a season. When it comes to studying the Bible, the most important questions are when, where, what and why. So set aside some time in your day: five, ten or a hundred minutes – it's up to you. Do you love getting up early for a run? Incorporate listening to the Bible into that. Do you have a long commute? Take a pocket Bible along with you. Are you a busy parent?

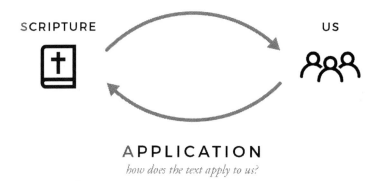

OBSERVATION

what does the text mean?

SCRIPTURE

US

APPLICATION

how does the text apply to us?

FIGURE 4: THE TWO QUESTIONS
OF HERMENEUTICS

Perhaps pick up the Word after bedtime (or before the kids wake up). Carry the same attitude to your Bible that you do to food – you need to eat; the question is when and where.

Three: Fight to find God

The primary way God speaks to us is through the Bible. Therefore, whatever it takes for you to get into your Bible, do it. If you find reading difficult, use an audio Bible. Can't be bothered? Wrong attitude. We're talking about getting to know Jesus here! Coeliacs don't just give up eating; they look for gluten-free food lest they starve. Be fervent and fight for a method that lets you engage with Scripture consistently. God has so much he wants to say to you, a pile of sin he wants to break in you and an infinite Spirit that he wants to forge in you. If your attitude to the Bible is ambivalent or blasé, you need to understand that you are cutting off the most vital line of communication with your Creator. It's time to do something about that.

OBSERVE

Whenever you open your Bible, you must ask two questions:

1.   What does the text mean?
2.   How does the text apply to us? (see figure 4).

The Bible is not a series of disjointed sentences. It's a library of books written by paupers and princes over 1,500 years in three different languages. Everything in the Bible was written by people from a different culture, who had a different alphabet and lived in a different era. To understand your Bible, you need to put yourself into the story. This is observation. The next three tips are principles of observation to help you get started:

Four: Read Slowly

Do not read the Bible as if it were a chore or tick list. Read slowly, thoughtfully and thoroughly. If you're reading and nothing is going in, slow down. Cherish every word, dig down deep for all the treasures of glory that God has placed for you to find. The gospel of Matthew is twenty-eight chapters long. An article on the Desiring God[6] website says it would probably take three hours to read the whole thing. I was in the book of Matthew for a year and loved it. There's no shame in taking your time.

Five: Know the Context

Every verse is part of a chapter, which is part of a book, which all fits into an overall story. For example, without context, when Jesus instructs people to drink his blood and eat his flesh (John 6:56), the application is rather awkward. With context, you see that Jesus was explaining to his Jewish brothers that he was the true Passover Lamb of God who was to be sacrificed so that their sin could be forgiven. A good way to start understanding the context is to read an entire chapter at a time.

Six: Don't forget the Big Picture

The Harry Potter saga was written by JK Rowling over the course of a decade, spanned seven books and has sold over one billion copies worldwide. That entire story can be summed up like this: Harry is the chosen wizard to rid the world of the evil Lord Voldemort. That means every book, character, side quest, relationship and conflict is part of that over-arching story. The same is true of the Bible: 'For God so loved the world that he gave his one and only Son, that whoever believes in him shall not perish but have eternal life' (John 3:16). The Old Testament points to Jesus and the New Testament is birthed from the life, death and resurrection of Jesus. There's one story, from which all other stories are born.

APPLICATION

Once you find yourself in the world of the Bible, from there you can see how the Bible is relevant to your world today. This is application. The following three tips will help you begin to apply the Word to your own life.

Seven: Get to know God

The Bible is about God and his acts in human history. It's the closest you'll get on this side of eternity to sitting at his feet. It reveals to you who God is and who God isn't. What pleases and angers God, as well as what excites and depresses him. The Bible lets you sit as close as you can to the maker of the rings of Saturn and so drink in as much of him as you can. Academics call this theology: the study of God. You should think of it as getting to know your heavenly Father.

Eight: Let God Change You

The Bible says that you are 'fearfully and wonderfully made' (Psalm 139:14). Let that seep in. Regardless of how you came into this world, God made you. God thought about you long before your parents ever did. Wherever you go, don't forget that you were designed by God for God. Be encouraged; you are the walking handiwork of God Almighty. However, the Bible also says, 'There is no one who seeks God. All have turned away' (Romans 3:12). That also refers to you. While we were each made by God, most of us pay him no attention, give him no glory and live as if he doesn't exist. Without Jesus, you are a sinner who will one day live in an eternity without God (just as you lived on earth). Let that sink in too. Do you see how the Bible is both encouraging and difficult? Don't let that deter you. Instead, repent. Think of yourself as a large block of marble. Think of the Bible as the chisel and the Holy Spirit as the sculptor. The more you read the Word and let it change you, the more permission you give him to chip away at the sin in your life, chiselling away at you until you are a perfect sculpture. Chiselling is painful. Chiselling is hard. But, one day soon, he will stand back, look at you, his perfectly fashioned masterpiece and say, 'Look what I have done. Look how astonishing she is! Look how marvellous he is!' Your repentance makes God look glorious.

Nine: Fulfil Your Mission

God doesn't only want to change your world; he wants to change the world through you. Jesus left us with one mission: make disciples locally, nationally and internationally (Matthew 28:18–20). However, as you read the Bible, you'll start to figure out how you can play your part in this mission. You'll start to see your specific purpose on earth more clearly.

To go back to Psalm 139, it was written by the greatest Jewish king in history, David. Isn't it interesting how David's song to God makes you feel great about yourself? Why? Because, although David's talking about himself being fearfully and wonderfully made, you realize that this truth also applies to you. Let's take that thought further. If that truth applies to you, doesn't it apply to everyone? Yes, but does everyone know that? This isn't just about you being fearfully and wonderfully made. This is also about all people, everywhere, being fearfully and wonderfully made. So, for those people that don't feel that way, doesn't your heart break a little bit? Aren't there millions of people all over the world, sitting right next door even, that don't feel special, unique or loved? For some Christians, their hearts break so much that they start organizations based exclusively on making people who struggle with self-worth feel that they are fearfully and wonderfully made. Jamie Tworkowski is one of those people. When Jamie met Renee Yohe, she was struggling with addiction, depression, self-injury and suicidal thoughts. He wrote about the five days he spent with her before she entered a treatment centre, and he sold T-shirts to help cover the cost. When she entered treatment, he posted the story on Myspace to give it a home. The name of the story was 'To Write Love on Her Arms'. Today, TWLOHA is a non-profit organization that has sent 200,000 messages and travelled over three million miles to meet people all over the world to tell them one message: you are fearfully and wonderfully made[7].

The point is this: as you read your Bible, the Holy Spirit will begin to encourage and inspire you. Who knows what adventures God wants to take you on as the Word prepares you for the world?

STOP & THINK

Abiding in the Bible. It's quite a tall order isn't it? First you must make a plan and then decide where you read it and when, being as consistent as possible to make it as regular as breathing. Which Potter fan ever did that? Ridiculous. Moreover, it's not as simple as reading the text; the Bible's not that straightforward. God lives between the lines.

Having done all that, you need to imagine yourself as a member of a foreign people, speaking a foreign language, in a foreign time. And obviously Jesus spoke plainly, right? Wrong. He used riddles, strange illustrations and parables. Good luck with that. From there you have to amass all the Saviour's words and put it in the wider story of the Bible, which just happens to span somewhere between 1–2,000 years.

To top it all off, you must take all that ancient information and make it relevant to you.

Breathe.

And then, after making it relevant, you can get a better grasp of the reason you were created in the first place, not to mention grow in your understanding of the creator himself.

Abiding in the Word *is* a horrifyingly impossible uphill struggle up Everest backwards, blindfolded and without oxygen. As you ascend the mount, the depths you'll discover about yourself, the brokenness of the world and the magnificence of God himself will be worth every early morning, every prayer and decision to forgo sleep or Netflix to open your Bible.

You'll need God at the start, as you simply won't be able to do it without him. But I promise, you'll see God at the end and God will carry you in the middle. That's why the last tip is simple: pray. Pray for discipline to make a plan. Pray whenever you see God show up. Pray when he seems absent. Pray when you can't be bothered, as well as when you feel passionate about it. Pray when it makes sense. Pray when it doesn't. Pray for the strength to make it a habit. Pray God breaks your heart. Pray he chisels away at your soul. Pray you don't abuse the text. Pray you learn to love the Bible but, more importantly, pray you learn to love the God behind it.

Think of the Bible as your oxygen tank.

Now go and read it. God's waiting for you.

RHYTHM

ABIDE IN YOUR BODY

3

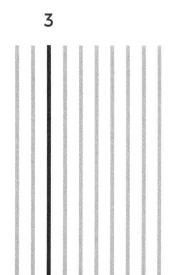

I write to you, not because you do not know the truth, but because you know it, and because no lie is of the truth...

Let what you heard from the beginning abide in you. If what you heard from the beginning abides in you, then you too will abide in the Son and in the Father.

And this is the promise that he made to us — eternal life.

1 John 2:21 & 24 – 25

My alarm goes off. I tap my phone to stop it. I then scroll through images and comments on social media. I tap my phone to like some of them. Then it's breakfast, a shower and scrubs for work (I'm a doctor). I tap again, this time to select my favourite playlist or podcast. I don the earphones and off I go. If I'm on the bus I will tap my phone a few more times to respond to messages, check the news, weather, my emails, bank balance and everything else. If I'm in the car, I sneakily tap while at the traffic lights. By the time I get to work, I've used my phone around twenty times.

Throughout the day, I continue to tap. In between seeing patients, I tap. After speak to their relatives, I tap. In between teaching, I tap. During lunch and, yes, even on the toilet, I tap away. Accessing messages, voice notes, social media. Big stuff. Little stuff. Important stuff. Dumb stuff. By five, I've probably tapped my phone 150 times. Then I get home, and tap to see the latest and greatest from all my friends, their friends and their friends. I tap to order some clothes, pay some bills and put on another playlist for the stereo while I cook dinner. Then, after some food, seeing friends and perhaps watching a film, it's off to bed. Then it's bedtime for the usual pre-slumber Instagram binge. By the time my head hits the pillow, I've racked up 200 phone taps.

Now before you start to sweat, don't worry, this chapter is not about smashing your phone. James KA Smith argues that ninety-five per cent of what we do is unconscious, meaning we are creatures of habit[8].

The above is a particular snapshot of my day. In reality, I spend most of my free time with Clare, most of my actual time at work and everything in between watching TV, writing and tapping my smartphone. God gets squeezed within the cracks: a little bit of time in the morning, some prayer before dinner but he doesn't feature much between dawn and dusk. It would seem that I'm being influenced more by my phone than the Holy Spirit.

UP, IN & OUT

3DM is a discipleship model developed by Mike Breen[9]. He noticed that disciples are made when they function in three dimensions: *Up*: with God & church; *In*: with a small community of people, where each can be known and grown; *Out*: serving the needs they encounter.

Mike noticed that this model produced more mature disciples, who had deep relationships as well as a strong commitment to serve their local areas. Up, In and Out is a simple and repeatable rhythm that creates battle-ready disciples. God, community, mission. Repeat. God, community, mission. Repeat. Over time that rhythm changes character and moves a person from baby to teenager to spiritual adult. Therefore, the remainder of this chapter will be looking at my version of creating 'Up, In and Out' within your life (figure 5).

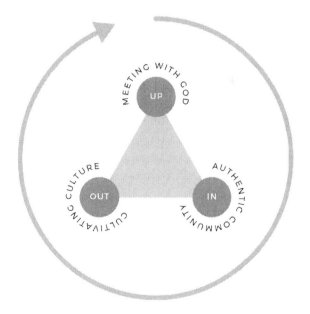

FIGURE 5: UP, IN AND OUT

UP: MEETING WITH GOD

Many people believe the universe did not occur by random chance but had a creator. Some call this creator a force, a 'higher power' or God. The creator made everything in the universe, from butterflies and fish to planets and galaxies. He did not just create this matter; God gave matter a function. God created planets as well as gravity, which keeps the planets in balance. God created flowers as well as photosynthesis, which lets plants make their own food. Without gravity, the sun would explode. Without photosynthesis, everything dies.

This rule also applies to us. God created food, money, science, music, beauty and love. Think about it: God made steak. I'll say it again: God made steak. While the carbon footprint from beef farming is large, and some people are offended by meat-eaters (in which case feel free to skip this sentence), there's a being that has let my tongue experience a medium rare fillet.

While we believe God created us to enjoy these wonderful gifts, God wants us to enjoy him even more. So, my praise doesn't only go to the chef, who did a great job preparing. Nor does it only go to the cow, who did a great job grazing[10]. My praise goes to the one who created them both.

But we are humans. Humans are short-sighted. We only see the steak and the chef.

We were made by God for God. In him are greater pleasures than anything we could have here on earth, for in God 'we live, and move and have our being' (Acts 17:28).

Therefore, creating 'Up' in your life is about taking your everyday actions and realizing that there's one who sits behind them all. So, eating isn't just eating; it's enjoying the fruits of his labour. Running isn't just running; it's embracing the muscles that God has created for your pleasure. At the heart of 'Up' is one principle: stop and think (which is why I make such a big deal about it at the end of each chapter). When we stop and realize that God is in all things, watching all things, at work in all things, whether good or tragic, that is when we learn to live in 'Up'. Steak is not just steak; it's savouring the genius of God. My work isn't just my work; God has given me the privilege of picking up a broom, typing on a keyboard or prescribing medication because he wants me to cultivate this world, just like he does. This is the essence of rhythm: developing habits that point us to what we love. Small, simple and repeatable habits that push us through the ceiling to the creator.

This is why Instagram is so addictive.

Tap, tap.

Easy habits.

Tap, tap.

Repeatable daily rhythms that slowly encourage us into using their app more each day. Don't get me wrong: Instagram is awesome. I use it, a lot. It's inspiring and funny. I send lots of messages on it, and think my life is improved by it. The same is true of Facebook and WhatsApp. (I guess I'm a sucker for anything made by Mark Zuckerberg). That said, my message is simple: let's at least give God the same level of attention that we give to our phones.

Although we have different jobs, our days tend to follow a similar pattern. We wake up, get ready, go to work, come home, get ready for bed and sleep. Somewhere in there is food, and somewhere in there is leisure. We may go to the gym, have kids to rear, homework to do or whatever. Most of our lives are on a predictable loop of habits – and *here* is where we need to burst through the ceiling. Here is where we take aim and develop a system of 'Up' by adding small, repeatable habits that point us to the King. To do this for yourself, there are two essential questions you must ask:

1. How do I connect with God?
2. When will I connect with God?

First the how. What stirs your affection for God? Here's a basic list to get you started: Reading the Bible, prayer, worship, study, meditation, silence. Take a discipline you love and make a small habit. A few minutes in prayer. A verse or section of scripture. Music that moves you. A moment of deep breathing. A time of study. Whatever you do that connects you to the Almighty, it must be small and repeatable. Again, Instagram's method is really simple – tap, tap. The more steps to your how, the less repeatable it is; therefore you'll do it less and will become more discouraged when you can't be bothered to do it.

Then comes the when – start with the morning. When I was younger, Christians were encouraged to have a 'quiet time' – morning time to read their Bible, pray, worship, light a candle etc. Although it's somewhat out of fashion today, it is still a fantastic way to start your day with God. Clare and I use our commutes for time with God as we pray for our (inevitably ridiculous) workdays ahead. I love listening to my Bible while I'm working out. Perhaps you could take a moment of prayer before eating, listen to some worship music while you're eating or a meditation while you're washing the dishes. Whatever it is, ensure it connects you to the Almighty and is small enough that you can do it most days of the week.

The how and the when is what determines the success of developing a system of 'Up'. As you learn to create your morning habit, then comes the time to let God invade the rest of your day. Before I was a doctor, I was a teacher, so, if there's one thing I know, it's a hectic workday. However, as busy as things can be, most of us get a break. Again, Instagram knows this and so during our five minutes of peace, we tap, tap. What would it look like for God to invade that space? That is the journey I'm on right now. Currently I'm working in rural Lincolnshire, within a small hospital in Grantham that has some incredible views of rolling farmland. My worktime habit is simple; during my walk from the ward to the canteen, I look out the window and take a few deep breaths. For those few precious seconds, I try to stop.

I stop thinking about my calendar.

About my patients.

About the emails I have yet to get to.

About dinner.

About the awkward conversation I had last week.

About everything…except him.

In…and out.

In the middle of the moment, I start to realize that, whether my day has been good or terrible, for those few beautiful moments, I'm finally aware that I'm breathing in the presence of God.

And then I move onto my jacket potato (and of course some tap, tap).

Small, enjoyable and repeatable. Time during the commute, and then time at lunch. I probably do this most days of the week, and it's an incredible way of letting God into the unconsciousness of my life. My next step is to create an evening routine, but the pull of Insta is just too strong, so pray for me. Now, it's your turn.

Pick a method.

Pick a time.

Enjoy creating a rhythm of 'Up' in your life.

FIGURE 6: CREATING 'UP' IN YOUR LIFE

IN: BUILDING COMMUNITY

In chapter one, we talked about forging an authentic community – a small group of people with whom you can be open and honest with. This is the second part of your rhythm, because your time with God should fill you with a love for people. As John reiterates again and again in his letter, we love God and people because he first loved us (more on this later). But, what does 'authentic community' mean? Our world is full of ways in which we can connect with one another, yet one fifth of the British population feels lonely, and two thirds of those nine million people are scared to admit it[11].

After years of research, popular sociologist Sherry Turkle surmised that our relationship with technology goes like this. We think technology will give us control, but technology ends up controlling us. Note that she discovered this at the dawn of the age of social media, in the noughties, with the ancient devices called Blackberries[12].

> We get Blackberries to better manage our email but find ourselves cradling them in bed first thing in the morning and last thing at night.

This is still so true today, in the age of the smartphone. Turkle goes onto say that our digital addiction means we struggle with analogue interactions – eg talking on the phone, having face to face conversations, resolving an argument without ghosting someone, going up to someone and asking them out on a date, etc. I know I hate at least two of those things and avoid them like the plague.

Our smartphones are changing us. Technology is making us the centre of our own universes, where we can craft our own digital world and let people see what we want them to see. So we curate and filter our profile photos – because even Jesus knows that the right filter can work miracles on our faces. We create our own political echo-chambers (you know, when everyone on your feed seems to vote left and you end up with a landslide victory for the right). We date whoever we want, however we want, on our own terms.

Our universe.

Our rules.

Our kingdom.

If you agitate our system, we unfriend you, block you, swipe left and erase you from our universe.

Sound familiar?

But, what's the result of this digital kingdom building? A significant increase in suicide rates increased for all groups of young people between 15 - 24[13]. Our curated digital worlds aren't working because, while everyone else may think they are real, we know they are false. We don't really look like that, we aren't really that confident and, deep down, we're really struggling. But it seems that death is better than giving up the gram, so where do we go from here?

Friends.

There's no magic formula to this one. You need friends. An authentic friendship has three elements to it: regularity, honesty and fun. That's the sweet zone. As I said in the preface, I'm a guy. Guys are masters of regular and fun community. *Goldeneye. Call of Duty.* 5-a-side. Darts. Wembley Doubles. Bookmakers. Gentleman's club. Pub. Arcade. Paintballing. Golf. *Final Fantasy.* We love to do stuff, and, while we do that stuff, we're not talking. So much of my life has been spent doing stuff with guys and never talking. Football for hours on a Saturday, but never talking about my insecurities, or how I'm struggling with my parents or whatever. I bet the same is true for most guys. If you try and bring honesty to your FIFA buddies, I'm pretty sure you'll be met with awkward pauses, dwindling thumbs and this hurried response, 'Yeah sounds difficult…Are you going to pass me the ball?' We can't handle it. And because we can't be honest, we make an awkward joke, laugh nervously and return to our comfort zone: regular and fun.

In my experience, girls love regular and honest. They seem more emotionally intelligent and, as a result, form more open friendships. Perhaps that's why suicide doesn't affect them as severely.

But, regardless of your gender, the ball is in your court. The task is simple: find a few friends to see regularly, have fun together and feel comfortable enough to be honest with. Jesus had three dudes in his inner circle. They saw him heal the sick, as well as have a nervous breakdown. Who's in yours?

OUT: LIVING MISSIONALLY

In the previous chapter, we looked at Jamie Tworkowski, founder of 'To Write Love On Her Arms', a non-profit company dedicated to presenting hope and finding help for people struggling with depression, addiction and self-harm. Why did he start TWLOHA?

Heartbreak.

When Jamie realized that many young people didn't know they were loved, his heart broke. He took his passion for people, made some T-shirts and went to music festivals, schools and universities. He heard their stories and signposted them to mental health professionals. Some celebrities started wearing his T-shirts and talk began to spread.

Eventually TWLOHA was given millions of dollars in donations and a film was made about its founding. However, the point is not the fame. Jamie's heartbreak has helped nearly 200,000 people worldwide. That's the point.

But what does this have to do with mission? Sadly, many Christians want to 'live for God', and so they instinctively enrol in official Christian ministry – church or Christian organizations. It's a subtle, but powerful idea: If you're not doing ministry, you're not really doing God's work. Nurses, screenwriters, lawyers, caterers, cleaners, secretaries and CEOs are only halfway there; the real glory is in the clergymen and women. This idea is better known as the 'sacred/secular divide'.

And it's nonsense.

The great reformer Martin Luther famously said that there is no difference between the ploughboy, the milkmaid and the priest – they all bring glory to God. Most of the heroes in the Bible weren't in professional ministry. Moses was a community organizer. Joshua was a commander. Saul was a soldier-turned-king. David was a labourer-songwriter-turned-king. Solomon – philosopher. Nehemiah – contractor. Esther – model. Ruth – farmhand. Joseph, Zerubbabel and Mordecai were governors. Matthew was a tax collector. Luke, a doctor. Paul, a tentmaker. Peter, Andrew, James and John were fishermen and Jesus was a carpenter.

Now that we've smashed the 'sacred/secular divide' to pieces, it's very important that you realize that, whatever your skillset, IQ, salary, heritage, race or address, God wants to change the world through you. Jesus left us with one mission: make disciples. But what does 'making disciples' mean? Love God and love people. By loving God and loving people, you make God look good.

That's the great mission.

That's our purpose.

That's what 'Out' means.

Therefore, what are the three things that help us discover our purpose?

Passion, skill and need. The intersection of those three elements helped Jamie find the inspiration for TWLOHA. That's how he made disciples. How do we discover our own passion, skills and needs? We ask three simple questions:

1. Passion: What breaks my heart?
2. Skill: What am I good at?
3. Need: What does the world need?

Let's start with passion. Are you ever bothered by stuff? Things you see or hear that just seem to annoy you? Niggles that you can't shake. Litter? Homeless people? Landfill sites? Maybe you find yourself thinking that the world would be better if a particular problem was solved? It can be 'big' stuff, like racial inequality or domestic violence. Or it could be 'little' stuff like poorly written children's books. Unsharpened pencils. Ugly buildings. Poorly chosen fonts on billboard signs. Badly organized spreadsheets or unhealthy school lunches in a canteen.

It gets to you doesn't it? Every time you drive past it, or see it or even think about it, it pesters you. Here's where the passion comes in. Don't push that feeling aside and just crack on with your day; let that feeling thrive. Let your heart be broken as you look at the world. Mourn over poor healthcare. Grieve backfiring cars. Lament jarring chord progression. Put simply: follow your tears.

You see, things that inspire us are fairly easy to come by, because they are celebrated. We put beautiful people on our TVs, inspiring people in our textbooks and royal people on our money. It takes a special set of eyes to look at the ugly.

Take heart, you haven't got those eyes by accident. God has let you see what my Pastor Malcolm Baxter calls the 'ashes' in the world[14]. God is a specialist at turning ashes into beauty, and your passion is found in the ugly – because it moves you to make it beautiful, if you let it. Therefore, ask yourself: what breaks my heart?

Next comes skill. Having been a teacher for five years and a youth worker for fifteen, I have discovered that, while school helps kids to excel academically, it does not help them develop their unique gifts and characteristics. Youth groups and friendships are much better at doing that.

Here's what I mean. I taught hundreds of kids from eleven to nineteen. Most of them left school with GCSEs, BTECs and A-levels; proof that they could do long division, memorize key dates or quote Shakespeare.

However, we didn't reward the kids who could calm a hostile classroom, make the Polish girl feel welcome or show great patience in dealing with annoying friends. It's not until you get into the workplace or have such people as your friends that you realize just how vital these 'soft skills' are to the success of any space you inhabit.

Therefore, when I start talking about skill, I'm not just referencing qualifications. Your skills are things that you are good at. Anything. It could be showing up on time, all the time. Making sandwiches. Playing football. Sparking conversation. Writing emails. Graphic design. Hosting parties. Driving. Analyzing data. Encouraging people.

I can think of three places you could find out what you're good at. The first is obvious: your CV. Trophies, certificates and degrees are the easiest way of saying that you are amazing at something. As I've mentioned, there are two more. Work and friends. Let's start with work. What do you get complimented for at school or in the office? What are you recognized at bringing to your workplace? It may not be something you put down on your resumé, but that skill is not an accident. Remember, there's no GCSE for attendance or consistency, yet these features are found in amazing employees.

The final place is your crew. Remember, your friends aren't your family. They don't have to hang around you; they do it by choice. Why is that? I didn't realize I was loyal until many of my crew said so. Clare is unbelievably consistent and reliable: it would take an act of God to keep her out of work or serving at church. But, she would be the first to say that she has thrived because people continually spur her on to do so. What are you good at? Go and look at your CV, ask friends in your workplace and talk to your mates. Make a list of your skills.

Finally, the need. Right now, one in ten children suffers with neglect. Comic Sans is still a widely used font. Four per cent of the British people don't have a job[15]. As you can see, our world is in desperate need. Kids need care. People need jobs and Comic Sans needs to die. What do people need around you? Do they need someone to talk to? A friend, a listening ear or some encouragement? Perhaps they need some education or upskilling to help them become more financially independent? Or do they need someone to create a really nice lamp so they can make their home beautiful?

Need is the gap in the world that your passion and skill hope to fill. If passion means looking at the ashes of the world, then need means looking at the beauty that can come from these ashes.

STOP & THINK

Now put it all together to create your life's rhythm: 'Up, In and Out'. Here is a reminder of the key questions or tasks to each part.

UP

- How do I connect with God?
- When will I connect with God?

IN

- Go and form relationships that have three elements: fun, regularity and honesty.

OUT

- Passion: What breaks your heart?
- Skill: What are you good at?
- Need: What does the world need?

My hope is simple. By going 'Up', you shall learn to live in constant communion with God, rather than stuffing him into the cracks of your hectic schedule. By going 'In', you shall form deep and enriching relationships where people know the real you, rather than your curated digital mask. Finally, by going 'Out', you will find ways, both big and small, in which you can use your passion and unique skillset to meet the needs around you.

God, community, mission. Repeat.

This is your rhythm for life.

TRUTH

ABIDE IN DISCERNMENT

4

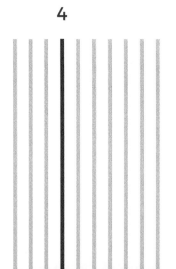

I write these things to you about those who are trying to deceive you.

But the anointing that you received from him abides in you, and you have no need that anyone should teach you.

But as his anointing teaches you about everything, and is true, and is no lie—just as it has taught you, abide in him.

1 John 2:26 - 27

At home, our parents preach sermons. At school, our teachers give us more sermons. The advertisements on every visible surface scream at us. Instagram, Facebook, Twitter et al love to throw in their two cents. Our smartphones, consoles and laptops constantly try to change how we walk, talk or dress. They scream at us: 'Buy this!' 'Sign up!' 'Feel that!' Church is not the only place you'll hear a sermon: you are in the middle of a hundred preaches from a hundred different directions. They all want a piece of you: your loyalty, your money or even your body. Some of these are true and should be embraced; others are false and should be rejected. So how do you know which is which?

Discernment.

Discernment is the power to tell whether something is true or false. How do we deal with this everyday carpet bombing of ads? The first option is acceptance: follow every message we hear. 'It's good to talk' – sign up with BT. 'Just do it' – buy some Nike trainers. 'YOLO' – get the tequila, some condoms and follow Drake's decadent lifestyle. But, let's just stop and think: this would mean we are constantly slaves to what we watch, see and hear. The second option is avoidance. No TV, no smartphone, no looking up when you see a billboard, closing your eyes on public transport, to say the least. It seems avoidance means you'd have to leave the world entirely, or become Amish. However, there is a third option: discernment. We listen to a given message, or story or advertisement and decide to receive or reject its truth. But how do we develop this skill?

God's Word and God's Spirit.

The Bible is a library of sixty-six books written in three different languages over a period of 1,500 years. As vast as it is, the Bible has one chief objective: to tell its readers about God. Paul puts it this way:

All Scripture is God-breathed and is useful for teaching, rebuking, correcting and training in righteousness, so that the servant of God may be thoroughly equipped for every good work – (2 Timothy 3:1–17).

While Jesus walked the earth, he was harassed by two enemies: Satan and the Pharisees. Luke 4:1–14, Matthew 4:1–11 and Mark 1:11–13 all document Jesus' temptation by Satan in the desert. The story goes like this: The Holy Spirit prompted Jesus to fast for forty days before starting his three-year ministry[16]. During his time in the wilderness, Satan continually asked Jesus to stop fasting and worship him instead of obeying God the Father. How did Jesus fight such temptation? Scripture.

During his ministry, Jesus had several run-ins with the Pharisees. When they accused him of being the devil, he used scripture (Matthew 12:24). When they said he was disobeying the Sabbath, he used scripture to show how they did not understand the point of it (Matthew 12:1–14, Luke 14:1–14).

Christians believe that, while human hands held the pen, God inspired the Bible. 2 Peter 1:20–21 says, 'No prophecy of Scripture came about by the prophet's own interpretation of things. For prophecy never had its origin in the human will, but prophets, though human, spoke from God as they were carried along by the Holy Spirit.' In addition, the Holy Spirit lives in every Christian; he is God within us (Ephesians 1:13). Jesus is the perfect example of a person both Word and Spirit. He lived by the power of the Spirit yet knew the Bible perfectly.

If Jesus needed the Word and Spirit, so do we. We cannot have big hearts and small heads: people that are 'Spirit-led' yet don't know a word of Bible. Neither can we have big heads and small hearts: scholars who have memorized the Bible in Ancient Greek yet have no day-by-day communion with God. We must have big heads and big hearts, as our Saviour showed us. By cultivating our intimacy with God and studying our Bible, we will grow in discernment.

BELIEVING LIES

Although we have God's Word (the Bible) and God himself (the Holy Spirit), why do we continue to believe lies? The answer is threefold:

1. Sin. We have a sinful nature; we don't know what God's Word says and we don't commune with him.
2. Satan. All Christians have a spiritual enemy who seeks to destroy our faith and will stop at nothing to do so.
3. Slothfulness. If we are lazy, we don't fill our minds with God's truth and dull our sense of hearing. Without the Spirit or the Bible, we put cotton wool in our spiritual ears.

Let's now try using the Word and the Spirit to help us overcome very common lies in the area of self-worth.

Lies about your self-worth

One of the greatest issues amongst my Gen Z and millennial generation is our understanding of self-worth. There are three factors that feed the modern Western mind: individualism, social media and the reverse-facing camera. Individualism says we are the most important voice in the room. Follow your truth. Choose your friends. Determine your gender. Sound familiar? Additionally, algorithms on social media highlight outrageous views i.e. it pays to polarise. Finally, a by-product of uploading selfie after selfie is that we begin to believe the world revolves around us.

But, the traffic is not flowing in one direction. Self-loathing is climbing as much as self-exaltation. Can you blame us? A third of girls have experienced sexual violence from a boyfriend[17] and 16,000 school absences per year are due to bullying[18]. Who needs enemies when so many of us are told, or shown, that we are worthless? Consequentially, self-harm, anxiety and depression have hit unprecedented heights. Worse still, there are four suicides per day for people between fifteen and thirty four, ¾ of which are by men[19]. It seems the world doesn't just push us to pride, it polarises our self-esteem. Some of us have delusions of grandeur. Others of us feel so worthless, we may as well end it all. At this point, we must ask: what does God think about us?

Truth #1: We Are All Equal

> Then God said, 'Let us make mankind in our image, in our likeness, so that they may rule over the fish of the sea and the birds in the sky, over the livestock and all the wild animals and over all the creatures that move along the ground.' So God created mankind in his own image, in the image of God he created them; male and female he created them – (Genesis 1:26–27).

Humankind was formed by God into God's image. This absolutely agrees with the universal declaration of Human Rights that 'all men are created equal'[20]. Therefore, we abide in that biblical truth – that every face on earth has equal worth because they were made Imago Dei (in the image of God). There's no race, ethnicity, age or class that is worth less or more than another.

We have the Word and now we must let it infest our spirit. Do you remember your reflection before prom, when you slipped on your first Air Maxes or finally got the offer? You felt like a diamond. What about the day she died, the time you did it again, or the date when he said 'It's over'? Worthless. Now, step back. Balance these two scenarios in your head: good days that leave you feeling great and the bad days that don't. Close your eyes and feel the happiness and the grief. Consider how the good day makes you feel good about yourself and how the bad day makes you feel about yourself. Look at the link between the day and your worth. The good boosts it; the bad saps it. Do you have it? Can you see it? It's almost invisible, but, like a spider's web in spring, you can see it in the right light.

That's the lie.

Every day we have things that raise our egos, and things that crush them. That's normal human emotion. Here's the lie: our feelings determine our worth. Now, let's pick up and wield the Sword of the Spirit (the Word): my worth is not determined by my esteem. Feelings can over- or under inflate us, so we must fight this lie with the truth. Whenever we come to God, we can say, 'Father, the world says that I'm awesome, but I'm not. I'm yours. The world says I'm worthless, but I'm not. I'm yours. Your opinion is the only one that counts. You made me in your image; I'm priceless in your eyes. May I believe your truth and not these lies.'

Truth #2: Humankind is fragile, but humankind is priceless

> When I consider the heavens, the work of your fingers,
> the moon and the stars, which you have set in place,
> what is mankind that you are mindful of them, human
> beings that you care for them? Yet you have made them a
> little lower than the angels and crowned them with glory
> and honour – (Psalm 8:3–5).

I remember reading and digesting these verses several years ago. In response, I have learned that we are not simply worthless bundles of cells. As his image bearers, we carry a small measure of his glory. We are little flecks of gold leaf shaved from a great statue. We are not grand like God; we are each a spoonful of atoms in a remote corner of a vast universe and here for milliseconds on history's timeline. Yet, as insignificant as we are, the being who fills every inch of the cosmos knows us intimately. He has bestowed honour upon us, knitted our DNA in our mother's womb, knows every hair on our heads, remains our constant and has loved us so much that in Christ he became a fleck of gold leaf.

Do you see how the Spirit takes the Word and not only makes it relevant, but turns it into your weapon? God's Spirit reinforces God's Word and God's Word reinforces the power of God's Spirit within.

Truth #3: God saves us by grace, not works

> All of us have become like one who is unclean, and all
> our righteous acts are like filthy rags – (Isaiah 64:6).

God is not impressed with our achievements; his feats are far more glorious. For those who feel that they are better than others, God says all our righteous acts are like filthy rags. God does not love us based on our performance, but because he is gracious. He doesn't love certain people more and others less – everyone can come to know God in Christ. There is no deed too dark that God could not forgive and no human act that God would reward with salvation. What a God we serve! We abide in God because he first loved us, not because we impressed him with our religion. Similarly, we can never say that we are worthless because we have God-given honour and glory. Regardless of what the world may say or do to us, we can never lose sight of the fact that the most powerful being in existence has clothed us in gold. I'll let God have the final word on this:

I tell you, do not worry about your life, what you will eat or drink; or about your body, what you will wear. Is not life more than food, and the body more than clothes? Look at the birds of the air; they do not sow or reap or store away in barns, and yet your heavenly Father feeds them. Are you not much more valuable than they? Can any one of you by worrying add a single to your life?

And why do you worry about clothes? See how they flowers of the field grow. They do not labour or spin. Yet I tell you that not even Solomon in all his was not dressed like one of these. If that is how God clothes the grass of the field, which is here today and tomorrow is thrown into the fire, will he not much more clothe you – you of little faith? So do not worry, saying, 'What shall we eat?' or 'What shall we drink?' or 'What shall we wear?' For pagans run after all these things, and your heavenly Father knows that you need them all. But seek first his kingdom and his righteousness, and all these things will be given to you as well. Therefore do not worry about tomorrow, for tomorrow will worry about itself. Each day has enough trouble of its own – (Matthew 6:25–34).

STOP & THINK

Three lies trip me up in all sorts of ways: 'My work determines my worth', 'I must not share my vulnerabilities because that will show that I'm weak' and 'I'm humble'.

Living in the truth means fighting against believing these lies. But it's a lifelong struggle. A constant, every day, back and forth. Sometimes I do well. Sometimes it's a shamble.

I work very hard, and so have to catch myself looking at why I'm working hard. Do I want to impress people? Do I want to please God? I'm naturally confident, and for a long time I thought being confident meant hiding all my flaws. Therefore, living in the truth means regular chats about how I'm doing. This might be easy for some of you, but it is really hard for me. Finally, I can fool myself into thinking I deserve God's love. I help young people, treat patients and recycle. Although nobody's perfect, I don't think I'm doing too bad. God has to bless me, right? The amount of times my pride has wrecked a conversation, or a moment, is countless. Living in truth means realizing that I place too much confidence in myself, and accepting people's criticism, as well as their praise, has been really healthy for me. As my crew are constantly saying to me, I have a big head. It needs shrinking.

****

Here is your task: write down three lies that you believe and answer the following questions.

1. Where do these lies come from?
2. What does believing each lie lead you to do, say and/or feel?
3. What do you need to do to help fight these lies? (If you're struggling with this one, ask a friend).

Diagnosis comes before treatment. A doctor needs to understand the patient's problem to give them the correct medicine. When it comes to growing in discernment, it's important that we first address the lies that we believe. By doing this task, you will have recognized the lies and come up with a battle plan to keep yourself abiding in the truth of God.

FATHER

ABIDE IN DAD

5

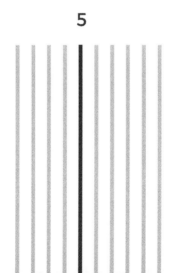

And now, little children, abide in him, so that when he appears we may have confidence and not shrink from him in shame at his coming. If you know that he is righteous, you may be sure that everyone who practices righteousness has been born of him.

See what kind of love the Father has given to us, that we should be called children of God; and so we are. The reason why the world does not know us is that it did not know him.

Beloved, we are God's children now, and what we will be has not yet appeared; but we know that when he appears we shall be like him, because we shall see him as he is. And everyone who thus hopes in him purifies himself as he is pure.

1 John 2:28 - 3:3

I want you to meet my friend Luke[21]. He lived on my street. When we were kids, Luke and his dad always went to West Ham football games together. Terry Thompson. He worked as a stamper at the Ford Dagenham plant until it closed down. A big burly bloke with a wide smile and a thick East London accent. Every Saturday, the two would be dressed in the full claret and blue kit, scarf tied and flag in hand. I'd watch green with envy from my window as the pair chanted the anthem 'I'm forever blowing bubbles' marching off to Upton Park Stadium.

After each game came Luke's full debrief: the banter on the tube, the police on horseback at the station and, eventually, the mediocre performance of the team. Those Saturdays were everything to him. Growing up, Luke's house was awesome: PlayStation, chicken nuggets for dinner and Coca-Cola on tap.

Then Terry was made redundant. They couldn't afford the ticket prices, so they went fortnightly, then monthly, then yearly, then not at all. Luke used to tell me his dad would work all over the place; he'd be gone for days. Days turned into weeks. Weeks turned into months. Finally, on the morning of Luke's 12th birthday, he left a note next to a classic West Ham kit, sponsored by Dagenham Motors: 'Happy birthday Luke. Sorry I couldn't be there, there's only work in Skeggy. When you're ready, come visit me.'

I'll never forget the tears as he read it to me again and again. The years that followed were hard. He blamed his mother for everything. His grades at school spiralled and he often fell asleep in class. Soon, he stopped watching football. Terry stopped sending cards.

Then we met Jake. Jake was a few years older than us. We had snuck into a pub under-age. Jake, knowing how out-of-place we appeared, bought us our first pints and kept our secret. He told us about life in East London: how to meet girls, get into clubs or make a bit of money.

Jake's story was a little like Luke's. Absentee father and several wayward teenage years. But he'd come out the other end because of an assisted living scheme for young people called Unlock. I'll never forget the look in Luke's eye. It said one thing: there's a way out.

Jake and Luke became good friends, and soon after that, Luke was gone. He packed his bag, left his mum and I didn't see him for years.

****

Dad. It's a word that conjures up so many emotions and memories, ranging from the affectionate to the abusive. According to the Centre of Social Justice, the family unit is the primary template from which we form all our other relationships[22]. This makes perfect sense: I engage with other people the way that my parents engaged with me. While no one would say that their parents are perfect, many people (including myself) would say that their parents or guardians tried to care for them. Some may not have made us feel particularly safe, others may not have been the most attentive, but most tried.

But is that true of both parents? Two out of three children born to cohabiting parents will experience the loss of at least one major attachment figure before the age of twelve[23]. Less than one in twenty couples are 'not in a relationship' at the time of a child's birth. By the time children reach the age of sixteen, around half will no longer be living with their dad. In short, between one and two million British children are not in meaningful contact with their father[24]. This leads to worse school outcomes and an increased likelihood that those children will live in poverty[25]. Therefore, for millions of young people both in Britain and abroad, it wasn't both parents that tried, it was only mum.

In this chapter, we'll be looking at the concept of God as our Father. The view of our earthly father colours the view of our heavenly Father and, in light of the statistics above, seeing God as Father can touch a deep and painful wound. I'm going to look at three keywords that will help us draw the line between God and our dad: creation, rescue and adoption.

CREATION

Our biological parents were our makers. They provided the cells, the womb and the home in which we were nurtured and raised. At the very least, our dads gave us half our DNA and without it, we wouldn't be here. When it comes to creation, whether your father was absent or dad of the year, that's as far as he goes, because he's human.

Before your conception, during your gestation and after your birth, God knew – and still knows – everything about you. He weaved you together as one fertilized cell multiplied to form organs and bones and skin. Then on your birthday, a pair of those organs inflated and out came your first cry. Psalm 139 puts this beautifully:

> For you [God] created my inmost being; you knit me together in my mother's womb. I praise you because I am fearfully and wonderfully made; your works are wonderful, I know that full well. My frame was not hidden from you when I was made in the secret place, when I was woven together in the depths of the earth. Your eyes saw my unformed body; all the days ordained for me were written in your book before one of them came to be – (Psalm 139:13–16).

You are not just a collection of atoms, but the uniquely crafted handiwork of the Almighty Creator of the universe[26]. Regardless of whether you have a disability, or are born into poverty, disease or discomfort, you are infinitely precious – the Imago Dei (image of God). A being made by God, with the breath of God, to the glory of God. Your body does not belong to you. You are his prize, the apple of his eye, the jewel in creation's crown. God made you; all your dad could do was wait.

While we are meant to live in harmony with God, he has given us choice – the option of whether we want to accept his love or not. One doesn't have to look very far to see the way humans treat themselves, their environments and other humans is not how God intended for us to live in his creation with these bodies he gave us (Romans 3:23). We are the children that spat in our heavenly Father's face; the lovers that cheated on our partners. Every time we rebel against what God wants – that's another rejection. Every time we think our laissez-faire religion is good enough for God, that's rejection. God gave us breath. Our response to such a gift? Rejection.

Another word for rejecting God is sin, and the apostle Paul says that the wages of sin are death (Romans 6:23), which means that sin is like smoking – eventually it will kill you. Ever since he breathed life into the children he crafted from stardust, our beloved Father has watched each one of us, from Mother Teresa to Donald Trump, slap away his hand and leave the eternal home for which we were made. Can you see the tears in his eyes as it happens again and again? Sin is not breaking God's commands, but breaking God's heart.

Our Big Misconception About God

Herein is where the main misconception about God as Father creeps in – too many of us believe that God is harsh. The stereotype goes like this: God's not fun, he's not understanding, he's sparingly merciful and ultimately…unkind. If God would ease up on the commands, get to know us and what life is like down here, then we would get on fine, but, as it stands, he's too harsh, too stiff and too violent for our taste.

Don't do this. Do that. Why must you always think x?
Why can't you start behaving like y?

If we believe this misconception, God becomes a cross between Gandalf the Grey, Thanos and Hitler ie a dry, sadistic, tyrant who is just itching for an excuse to punish you. And how do you know whether you believe this or not? Our response is either religion or rebellion. If you're religious, you approach God with shame.

I swore. I stole. I wounded. I got drunk and so I'm
ashamed.

Religious people recognize that they are unholy, and God is the perfect embodiment of holiness. We've all felt a glimpse of this, because everyone knows what it feels like to be caught with your hand in the cookie jar. The religious live there. They feel guilty and condemned because they just aren't good enough, no matter how hard they try.

On the other hand, if you're rebellious, you don't approach God at all. Rebels put their middle finger to heaven and walk away.

I swore. I stole. I wounded. I got drunk and so what?
I don't care. You tell a lie, sleep with Staci or give your
brother a wedgie and all the sudden you find yourself in
hell? What a joke.

The rebellious also realize that they are unable to fulfil all God's commands, but don't approach God at all. The rebellious recognize that they are unholy, and God's standards are impossible to attain, so don't bother.

I think most of us fit somewhere along this line. Both our rebellion and religion arise from an incorrect perspective of God. We see God wrongly; this chapter is about restoring our sight. What is the cure to being someone that either rebels or becomes religious? Realizing that God has rescued and adopted you.

RESCUE

God's reaction to our rejection is rescue. If the shoe was on the other foot, I don't know if I'd have the same reaction as God. If I held the cosmos in my right hand, I wouldn't be as gracious to such ungrateful children. Earthly fathers are judgemental; God is merciful.

The mark of a good parent is initiative; they act first. They love you, help you and rescue you, in spite of whether you ask for help or not. How many children ask for a nappy change? The list of things that I've done to my mum is astounding, and yet she still loves me just as much as the day she gave birth to me. I've urinated on her. Kissed her. Pooed on her[27]. Hit her. Screamed at her. Hugged her. Cried on her. Wrestled her. Slept on her. Likewise, God's rescue didn't come because I asked for help or sent out an SOS. God acted first.

God's initiative looks like incarnation. Incarnation is Latin for 'in flesh'. When Jesus came into the world, he repeatedly said that he was sent by God the Father to a world that would reject him (John 6). When Jesus was born, theologians say that God became incarnate, ie flesh and bone. That's why we make such a big deal about Christmas (Jesus' birth) because it's proof that God planned to rescue me before I ever loved him back. People only realize they are sinners long after they start sinning, which means he put up with my mess long before I realized I had any.

ADOPTION

God's plan to rescue us was not simply about Jesus coming to live among us. There's the whole sin issue. Let me put it a different way: why do we love justice? Because we believe in right and wrong. If someone murdered your uncle in cold blood, you'd like that person to be punished. That would be just. Sadly we live in a world where two per cent of people have ninety-eight per cent of the resources, sexism is still a thing and one in ten children are abused[28]. In other words, justice is a nice idea, but may be an unobtainable reality that humankind aspires to but never reaches. What if there was a being that was perfectly just? Someone who didn't have to collect evidence, gather witnesses or refer to any authority to punish those that promote injustice?

God is omnipotent and omnipresent. That means that he is all powerful and everywhere at once. God doesn't just know our sin; he was there watching us do it. He's not reviewing CCTV footage; he was an eyewitness. He doesn't need permission, requires no council and is the biggest advocate for justice in the universe. He makes UNICEF look like terrorists and charities look like drug rings. If God really is just, he can't let us into the Kingdom. If treason is punishable by death, how can he let us off the hook with a slap on the wrist? He must put us in the stocks. A life of sin not only proves that hell is what we deserve, it's proof of what we wanted in the first place – a life without God.

Here's where it gets ridiculous. I am a sinner, a man that rejects God and does whatever he wants. Amidst all that selfishness, he died for me. At my worst, God did his best. He took the entire catalogue of my sin: every rejection, every rebellion and every act of religion – and then he forgave me. He paid the price I could never pay. In Jesus, God set forth his plan of redemption. The cross is a blazing symbol across time that God decided to rescue you. With the tears still fresh on his cheeks, God put on his coat and left his home to find you.

> This is love: not that we loved God, but that he loved us
> and sent his Son as an atoning sacrifice for our sins – (1

John 4:10).

There it is; the beauty of the cross. The cross was a symbol that the Romans regarded as disgusting. When a Roman heard 'crucifixion', they got the same gut-turning feeling that you or I get when we hear 'Auschwitz'. How then, did this symbol become the blazing badge of Christianity?

Adoption. The cross is the gateway back into the family of God. Jesus' death cancelled any debt, any crime, any guilt, any payment or any problem between us and our heavenly Father. The one whom we wronged, slighted and spat at did not count it against us but put it all on his Son just so we could we welcomed home. What a ridiculous kind of love! That's why John gets so excited.

> See what great love the Father has lavished on us, that we should be called children of God! And that is what we are! – (1 John 3:1).

God didn't need us, yet he paid the ultimate price just to have us. He made us, we rejected him and yet he came back to bring us home. Why? Because of one of the most wonderful words in the dictionary – grace.

GRACE

If God did not judge evil, then he most certainly would not be good. He doesn't side-step it, sweep it under the rug or just make it disappear. Right now, he is gathering every insult, fit of rage, murder, white lie, rape, illegal download, theft, wayward thought, act of paedophilia, condescending glance, genocide, etcetera.

Etcetera is an interesting term. It's Latin for 'and the rest'. When you think about it, etcetera represents a long list of stuff that's so numerous that it would be too tedious and time consuming to write it out. If I were to unpack your bag of etcetera, would I have enough room to display all your mess? Enough pages of paper to list every thought, word or deed?

No.

None of us do.

Yet, God is collecting our etcetera as articles of evidence in a case.

A case?

Yes.

A case against you and I.

In other words, a judgement.

God does not judge us because he has a short fuse, or because we have made minor errors. God judges us because for as long as we have been breathing oxygen we have repeatedly rejected his outstretched hands, wronged other human beings and done it all with the same idiom on our lips: nobody's perfect. God sees injustice and is too loving to simply let it be. However, the news is not all bleak. God has shown us the greatest example of mercy in Jesus Christ.

> God sacrificed Jesus on the altar of the world to clear
> that world of sin. Having faith in him sets us in the clear
> – (Romans 3:25, *The Message*).

To see the heights of God's mercy, we need to see how far we have fallen. Scripture acts as a mirror and a medicine. God wants us to realize that we are great sinners, but he is an even greater Saviour. For every etcetera, God paid the price. He stacked every piece of evidence in a case against himself. The pinnacle of God's judgement is seen in Jesus on the cross, where God placed every sin that we committed and judged his son in our place. What do you call something you completely didn't deserve?

Grace.

It's the unmerited favour of God. You could not earn it through religion or buy it over the counter, yet you could not stand before God without it. Grace makes my heart sing when it is down, for who else found me at the bottom of the ocean? Grace lifts me from my battered self-esteem, for no earthly king ever gave up their throne to find me. Grace makes him look so beautiful, for who else could pay my etcetera? Grace completely transforms my view of myself and my God.

> Amazing Grace, how sweet the sound that saved a wretch like me – John Newton, 1779.

Jesus said, 'Blessed are the poor in spirit' (Matthew 5:3). Another word for people who are poor in spirit is wretched. Why? Wretches realize they need grace.

STOP & THINK

To finish this section, I want to share a story that I made up about Luke. Remember, Terry left Luke to live in Skegness while he went to Unlock. I share it because it summarizes exactly what I want this chapter to leave you with: a change in perspective.

****

He jumped over the bin and continued to run. He could see the end of

Trundle Street up ahead. If he took a left and raced down the alley, she'd never catch him. 'Heighton Road?' he thought, gazing at the sign as he scrambled across the street. 'That's on the other si–!'

The oncoming Fiesta struck his leg and threw him against the kerb. Any faster and he'd have needed an ambulance. As the young driver wiped the tears of shock from her eyes, he clambered to his feet and limped up the hill into the nearby wood. He didn't have time to check himself over.

She was close.

He was lost.

The trees were tall and bulky. The thick canopy shrouded the woodland floor, so Luke tucked himself into a nook among two shrubs. After a silent four minutes came the familiar metal clink. His body was still; his mind wasn't. 'Jake's gone. Poor Isaac only lasted a few days. I had to run, or she'd get me too. In this business, if you don't run, you disappear.'

The foot landed two inches from his nose. A drop of her sweat graced his forehead as she hovered above him. She was tired, but she was tenacious. She scanned the wood, moving from one part of the forest to the next systematically. He was well hidden, but the pain was getting worse.

Seeing her in the distance, Luke retreated from the cranny, turned and hobbled in the opposite direction. Unable to lift his right leg properly, he staggered on, tripping on logs and ripping his clothes on thorns and thistles. Nothing was going to stop his escape.

After what seemed like hours, he neared the edge of the wood. The pain had turned to drowsiness. He glanced beyond the canopy at the bus stop. 'Three pounds should get me to T's house. Good thing I bought a fiver.'

The passengers winced at his odour as he made his way to the back of the bus. Covered in bruises and clothed in shreds, he looked like he'd lost a fight to an oak tree. He sat down gingerly, as thoughts of a fish and chips dinner blocked out the surrounding judgments. Drowsiness gave way to slumber and he closed his eyes for the two-hour trip back to Skegness.

'End of the line.'

Feeling rejuvenated, Luke limped to his feet and headed for the exit.

'That's the furthest you've ever got.' Turning around, he could make out her silhouette. She must've been sitting in the row in front the entire time. 'Your leg'll be fine. The injection should get rid of the pain and the bandage will help.' He peered down to see a full set of clean dressings around his right calf. 'You're really going back to Terry? The man who couldn't be bothered to feed you so gave you chicken nuggets every night.' She got out of her seat and started towards him. 'Do you know why you've got that scar on your forehead? When you were two, your dad got drunk and left the first-floor window open.' Luke felt the contours on his scalp. 'You nearly died on the operating table, but we could never charge him with neglect 'cos there wasn't enough evidence.' As she drew closer, her voice grew softer. 'It wasn't until he threw your mother out a moving car that we were able to send him down.'

His anger started to bubble. 'And why should I stay wit' yous lot? Where's Jake? You think you're sick 'cos you take us in, put Primark on our back and get us a couple GCSEs. Then you boot us out the door and call it 'care'.' Luke's voice broke. 'You're all the same. At least Terry admits he was a prick.'

Rachel sniggered. 'Four times. That's how many times Isaac ran away from me. He always ended up at the corner shop, realized he had nowhere to go, and turned around. Jake was a bit harder. Before you got here, he once spent an entire week camping in the woods you were in earlier till we found him shivering and eating a used Pot Noodle. You, however Mr Thompson have taken the record: one hundred miles.' She took the chain of keys from out of her pocket. 'The way we work at Unlock is very simple. We'll feed you. We'll clothe you. We'll teach you and we'll let you go. We will give you the life that you were supposed to have.' She unfastened a bronze key and placed it in Luke's palm. 'When you successfully pass your exams, we send you off to your new apartment where you'll start your new job.' She clasped his hand and lifted his chin with the other. 'Jake and Isaac are waiting for you. You ran out the centre before you even opened the envelope. In any case, let me be the first to say it: well done young man.'

Through the tears, Luke glanced down as Rachel handed him the manila envelope. Passes in BTEC Science, Engineering, English and Maths.

'Unlock is finished. You can stay on this bus with me and go back home to pack. Or you can go back to Terry. The choice is yours.

****

Regardless of how wonderful or terrible they may be, all our earthly fathers are imperfect men. We take those lenses and make God a macro-version of dad. No wonder we are hesitant to approach him, talk to him or surrender our lives to him – he's literally a massive disappointment. Or so we assume. Abiding in the Father means that I live in full light of these truths: he made me, I rejected him, he rescued me by spilling his own blood and all because he continually loves me.

The purpose of this chapter was to correct our perspective of God.

We should not judge heaven by earthly standards, but rather do the opposite. Just like Luke's dad, Terry Thompson, our earthly fathers fall tremendously short of the perfect love found in the Father. My dad did not create me, God did. My dad sinned against me, God didn't. My dad punished me according to my sins against him; God punished himself for my shortcomings. My dad loved me imperfectly; God's love completed me. My dad tried to be just; God is just. I thank my earthly father for doing all that he did – but he was always going to fall short. I forgive him for his failures and hope that my children will do the same for me.

Since this chapter is about contrasting our heavenly and earthly fathers, here's your task (which it would be best for you to do alone): spend a few minutes in silence thinking about your dad. Then spend a few moments thinking about God: his character, his attributes etc. As both images come to mind, here are some questions to think about:

1. What do you think about your earthly dad?
2. What comes to mind when you think of God the Father? Why?
3. Do you think you are prone to judging your heavenly Father by your earthly father's standards?
4. How has your perception of God changed as you've read this chapter?

WAR

DO NOT ABIDE IN SIN

6

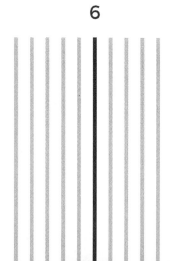

Everyone who makes a practice of sinning also practices lawlessness; sin is lawlessness. You know that he appeared to take away sins, and in him there is no sin. No one who abides in him keeps on sinning; no one who keeps on sinning has either seen him or known him.

Little children, let no one deceive you. Whoever practices righteousness is righteous, as he is righteous.

Whoever makes a practice of sinning is of the devil, for the devil has been sinning from the beginning.

The reason the Son of God appeared was to destroy the works of the devil. No one born of God makes a practice of sinning, for God's seed abides in him; and he cannot keep on sinning, because he has been born of God.

1 John 3:4 – 3:9

Everything is made of atoms. Nevertheless, atomic structure remains a complex area of science. The mantra we use at school is that an atom has neutrons and protons in the middle with electrons orbiting them both. While that's correct, that is merely scratching the surface. There are so many theories, experiments and discussions about atoms that it seems as if we'll never fully grasp the fundamental substance from which everything in the universe is made. Understanding sin is about as easy as understanding atoms.

CHILDREN OF THE DEVIL

When I say the word 'Satan', what comes to mind? Heads turning all the way around? Halloween? Tridents? Angels? The Exorcist? To us in the West, the words Satan, the devil or Lucifer conjure extreme and crazy quasi-religious activities that most people would never participate in. Whenever the word 'Satan' is mentioned, most people in the secular, post-modern West don't have a sense of fear or dread, because Satan belongs in the same pile as Ouija boards, horoscopes and witchcraft – paranormal elements from tabloid newspapers, children's nightmares or psychiatric units.

You are a child of Satan.

Yup...I know.

This isn't *Paranormal Activity 5* or a Stephen King novel, the Bible calls all sinners (ie all human beings), children of the devil. Understandably, you're probably looking for an explanation for such an insane statement, so here goes.

God is perfect. As mentioned in the previous chapter, we are the apex of his creation – uniquely crafted image bearers. He wanted all human beings to be shining reflections of him. Starting with Adam and Eve, and including us, humans continue to disobey God. We live autonomously: worshipping whatever we want; spending money however we want; sleeping with whomever we want. The list continues. We even do things that offend our own consciences, let alone God's: we abuse power, plunder the earth's resources for profit and wage unjust wars. From the smallest to the largest of offences, sin is anything that goes against God's intention for his creation. He made us to be perfect; we tainted that perfection like a drop of milk in a glass of water.

Deepak Chopra would argue that the reason world hunger and inequality still exists is because we have not achieved self-actualization and enlightenment[29]. Most governments agree that such evil exists because we haven't discovered the right technology or educated enough people to overcome these problems. They create policy and make laws to improve society, yet from the dawn of civilization in Egypt to the UN, our world is still plagued by many ills.

The Bible has a different take on it. Behind every sin, from white lies to genocide, lies a tempter; a small voice in our ears that persuades us to sin. An external force or being that is, in part, responsible for every act of evil in the world. This being's name is Satan, but is also known as the devil, Lucifer or the enemy.

CHILDREN OF GOD

What does God have to say? How does God feel about the pinnacle of his creation being taken hostage by the prince of darkness? He does not simply leave us to die in our mess but brings us home.

Jesus takes those who have been walking in darkness and makes them children of God. This is known as the doctrine of regeneration, but you've probably heard it referred to as being 'born again' or 'finding God'. This is a particularly important point. A Christian is someone that recognizes that they used to be a sinner and now God has made them a saint. He completely transforms our nature, taking us back to his original intention.

All Your Sin Has Been Forgiven

Read what the subheading says again: 'all your sin has been forgiven'. There are three especially important terms here: all, your sin and forgiven.

- *All:* Jesus' death on the cross doesn't just mean that all your past sin has been forgiven. His crucifixion atoned for past, present and future sin.
- *Your sin:* If you were the only person on earth to have ever sinned, Jesus would still have had to get off his throne in heaven, enter human history as a man and die the most brutal death imaginable just for you. That's how serious sin is. Think of all the things you have thought, said and done. Think of the amount of grief, heartache and strife you have caused God.
- *Forgiven:* Dwell on and be pained by your sin...and then look to the cross, for Jesus paid for it all. It will never count against you again. His blood has wiped away every blemish and now you stand before God as white as snow. Amazing grace, how sweet the sound, that continues to save wretches and make them saints.

YOU STILL SIN

Although Jesus died for all our sins: past, present and future, we still sin...continuously (or maybe it's just me). From what John implies, there are two trajectories of sin that indicate whether you abide in God or Satan. On the one hand, the righteous man strives to practice righteousness and fight the urge to practice sin. The unrighteous man recognizes that he is sinful but doesn't care.

> Shall we go on sinning, so that grace may increase? By no means! We are those who have died to sin; how can we live in it any longer? – (Romans 6:1).

Why does this phenomenon exist? God's Spirit abides in the righteous. Therefore, to the righteous, sin is something they get drawn into, trapped by and, ultimately, hate. Though they may find it pleasurable for a moment, sin makes them miserable as they defame the holy God that lives inside them. Have you ever been caught in a sin and felt a gnawing inside of you? That's God nudging your conscience, saying, 'This goes against your very nature!' My old pastor used to call the Holy Spirit 'the hound of heaven' because he will not let us go, especially in times of sin. Sure, we can try and drown out the Spirit, but he has a knack for chipping away at our conscience, making sin as unbearable as possible.

The unrighteous man can live in sin with no qualms. Why?

God does not abide in him.

How scary a prospect that God, knowing how deadly sin is, allows people to get what they really want, the prize of sin – a life and eternity without him.

FIGHT THE THREE ENEMIES

The Christian is in a war. On the one hand, the Holy Spirit is always helping, guiding, convicting and encouraging us to live a godlier life day by day. But the Christian has also made new enemies: the world, the flesh and the devil.

One: The World

In AD 50, the Apostle Paul founded a church in Thessalonica[30]. Thessalonica was a major Greco-Roman coastal city with significant military, economic and political assets, so when you think of it, think LA, Sydney or Barcelona. The church's members were composed of previously devout Jews and Greeks. Paul wrote 1 and 2 Thessalonians because it was under fierce persecution from Jews and Greeks outside the church (see 1 Thessalonians 2:15).

There was Jewish pressure for the Christians to stop worshipping Jesus as the Messiah. From the other side, traditional Greeks scoffed at these 'born again' Greeks, jibing them with statements like: 'Are you actually serious about this Jesus thing?', 'It's your body, do what you want!', 'What would your family say?', 'Worship Jesus and we'll disown you.'

Sound familiar?

When the term 'world' is used negatively in the Bible, it is referring to a culture that does not honour God. These are the messages we hear at work, school and in our home, from friends, family and colleagues who discourage us from following God. Whether they know it or not, they are ruled by and submit to Satan's power, because they stand so contrary to the truth.

Jesus said, 'In this world you will have trouble. But take heart! I have overcome the world' (John 16:33). Jesus also said, 'Whoever wants to be my disciple must deny themselves and take up their cross daily and follow me' (Matthew 16:24). Followers of Jesus are destined for difficult trials, during which there is constant and sustained pressure to veer us off track. We should not be surprised by it, nor overwhelmed, for, while the world is powerful, the Holy Spirit is more so.

Two: The Flesh

Sometimes the chaos in my head is the scariest place to be. Although I may know the right thing to do, there's always a burning desire to do wrong. My pillow can be an uncomfortable place. 'I know God said wait till marriage, but she's so hot', 'I know I should forgive him, but I can't', 'I know we're equal, but they're immigrants.'

Are you like me? Don't you want to scratch the itch? You know it'll feel better for a moment. You know it'll feel good. But you also know it's the wrong thing to do.

The term 'flesh' refers to the sinful nature of every human being (Galatians 5:19–21). If the world is the enemy without, the flesh is the enemy within. The flesh wars against our spirit, compelling us to satisfy our base desires. This battle is raging in all Christians, all the time. One in ten people struggle to control their anger[31]. Flesh. Right now, 30,000 people are watching online porn[32]. Flesh. Sometimes we lose battles to the flesh: we post that comment, click that thumbnail, say that word, do that thing, think that thought – and the list goes on. We feel good for a second, but our consciences catch up soon enough.

The Christian should think of this war with the flesh as precisely that, a war. In any war, there are many battles, but only one victor. Peter was a coward, denying Jesus when accused by a servant girl (Luke 22:54–62). And yet he finished his days with such courage, even though he was crucified upside down. Although Paul struggled with a 'thorn in the flesh' (2 Corinthians 12:7–10), he became the greatest church planter in history. Martin Luther hated Jews. He died as the founder of the Protestant movement. Martin Luther King Jr had numerous extramarital affairs. He died as the greatest black rights activist ever. Flesh, flesh and more flesh. All these men were Christians, not the pre-Jesus version. They were the hand-raising, Jesus-loving, Bible-believing pillars of the faith. These men are our heroes, yet they too lost battles to the flesh, scratching the forbidden itch.

Here's the bad news: you will lose many battles to the flesh. Here's the good news: the Holy Spirit will win the war. Take heart: you will win far more battles than you lose for he is our spiritual surgeon, making us new from the inside out. Like any invasive procedure, this process is painful but beneficial. He sees your sin, doubt, anger mismanagement, unbelief, bitterness, prejudice, sexual deviances, apathy, unforgiveness, selfishness, the sins of your past and the sins of your future. He shines his light on your mess and picks up the knife. He will remove the cancer of sin, but it won't be quick; this process will take a lifetime. We will not be perfect until we are in glory.

Three: The Devil

Satan is regularly referred to as the adversary, the enemy, the devil or the tempter. In essence, Satan is a being that traps people into behaviours or situations that hinder their relationship with God or bring them to harm. Yes, we are responsible for our sin, but Satan continually looks to widen the chasm between us and God. Satan's work started in the garden of Eden (Genesis 3:1) and, since then, has had devastating consequences for all humankind: poverty, abuse, war, divorce, bullying, lying, pride, religiosity, idolatry etc. Every conceivable evil in this world is a direct result of the work of Satan.

That said, as mighty as the acts of Satan are, there is another who is more powerful. Why God allows Satan to roam for the time being and cause so much suffering we cannot answer. What we most assuredly can say is that these afflictions are momentary. Take heart for Jesus said many times that there will be a final judgement of both demons and Satan himself (Matthew 25:41).

STOP & THINK

What happens in our heads and hearts that we so quickly forget the Gospel that took us from death to life? The answer is simple – there's a battle for truth. This battle rages within our heads and our hearts. While we cling to the truth of the Gospel, there are constant threats to it: our flesh wages war. The world is constantly preaching the anti-Gospel. These sermons are in our advertising, our music, our newspapers, our films and our conversations. The cultural air we breathe undermines and confuses our view of the Gospel. Lastly there's the devil. Satan makes it his business to find Christians and corrupt our view of God and his beautiful Gospel by whispering untruths and heresies in our ear, just as he did to Adam and Eve.

For the Christian, sin is something that they hate doing. The Bible calls this conviction, and, while it doesn't feel great, it's extremely helpful. To grow as a Christian, listen to the conviction of the Holy Spirit, as well as the wisdom of trusted friends. This will lead you to repentance and help you to live differently.

Therefore, to grow in your war against sin, you need God, people and a whole heap of grace. Never, ever, ever forget that Jesus paid for all your sin: past, present and future. Here's your task: get a date in with a close friend and discuss these nice juicy questions:

1. How does your 'flesh' lead you into sin? How does your friend's flesh lead them into sin?
2. How does the 'world' lead you into sin? How about your friend?
3. How does Satan lead you into sin? And your friend?

We are all fighting the war on three fronts, yet many Christians fight alone. As John Watson says, 'Be kind, for everyone you meet is fighting a hard battle'[33]. The Christian life doesn't make sense unless the church is family; the fellowship of people that God is working within and weaving together. Sin, death and Satan stalk us, which means I need you as much as you need me as much as we all need him.

I am my brother's keeper. Yet, I still struggle with this today. I hate asking for help. I hate showing that I'm weak. My independence always wants to fly solo. Repentance for me looks like surrounding myself with Clare and my friends, who help me, struggle with me, call me out and lean on me as I lean on them. That's how you fight sin.

Christian, pick up your arms.

Schedule that chat and win your war.

POWER

ABIDE IN THE SPIRIT

7

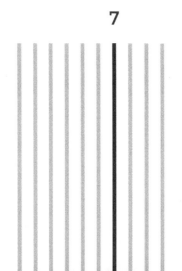

But if anyone has the world's goods and sees his brother in need, yet closes his heart against him, how does God's love abide in him?

Little children let us not love in word or talk but in deed and in truth. By this we shall know that we are of the truth and reassure our heart before him; for whenever our heart condemns us, God is greater than our heart, and he knows everything.

Beloved, if our heart does not condemn us, we have confidence before God; and whatever we ask we receive from him, because we keep his commandments and do what pleases him. And this is his commandment, that we believe in the name of his Son Jesus Christ and love one another, just as he has commanded us.

Whoever keeps his commandments abides in God, and God in him. And by this we know that he abides in us, by the Spirit whom he has given us.

1 John 3:17-24

Most of the time, the Christian faith makes sense. As scandalous as it sounds, the all-powerful God sees his creation rejecting his commands. Instead of destroying them, he enters their world, patiently teaches them how to live and makes the ultimate sacrifice so that he may enjoy their company for the rest of eternity by atoning for their treason. Again, scandalous, but it makes sense.

However, there are aspects of the Christian faith that cannot be so easily explained. One of them is obedience. The Bible is full of commands from God that we, as Christians, ought to obey. John goes as far as this, 'Whoever claims to live in him must live as Jesus did' (1 John 2:6). Jesus presses harder:

> If you do not remain in me, you are like a branch that is thrown away and withers; such branches are picked up, thrown into the fire and burned.
>
> If you remain in me, and my words remain in you, ask whatever you wish, and it will be done for you. This is to my Father's glory, that you bear much fruit, showing yourself to be my disciples.
>
> As the Father has loved me, so have I loved you. Now remain in my love.
>
> If you keep my commands, you will remain in my love, just as I have kept my Father's commands and remain in his love – (John 15:6–10).

Jesus says our obedience proves that we are abiding in God. Therefore, if we follow this system logically, you can begin to think that the more you follow his commands, the more God will be pleased with you. It's at this point that things start to get confusing.

UNRIGHTEOUS OBEDIENCE: RELIGION

The most obedient people in the Bible rolled in the same crew – the Pharisees. They kept God's Law so well that they would not only donate their money but gifts and even their spices. (Can you imagine donating a portion of your paprika?!) They'd fast twice a week, memorize their whole Bible and so much more. Their obedience was meticulously perfect. However, Jesus despised the heart behind their obedience:

> Woe to you, teachers of the law and Pharisees, you hypocrites! You are like whitewashed tombs, which look beautiful on the outside, but on the inside are full of the bones of the dead and everything unclean. In the same way, on the outside you appear to people as righteous, but on the inside you are full of hypocrisy and wickedness – (Matthew 23:27–28).

Much of Jesus' and the Pharisees' everyday routines were very similar. The Pharisees taught the Scriptures, as did Jesus. Both parties had disciples, worked with the poor, healed people, participated in religious holidays and were pillars of the Jewish community. However, Jesus so hated their faith that he warned others about how damaging it was to follow them. In other words, the Pharisees obeyed God's Law for all the wrong reasons. Jesus was just as obedient as the Pharisees but obeyed God for the right reasons (see table 1).

Every Christian must obey God, but there's a way that's righteous – and a way that is unrighteous. People that are religious think they are holy because of their actions, not because it is God who has made them holy. Religious people want to show off their devotion because they prefer the applause of people to the applause of God. Ultimately, religious people think they deserve God's blessing, whether it be through money, peace or eternity. Religion rejects the undeserving grace of God because

ACT	WHAT DID THE PHARISEES DO?	WHY?	WHAT DID JESUS DO?	WHY?
PRAYER	Prayed long and complex prayers in public (Matt 6:5)	So their prayers could be seen and heard by others (Matt 23:5)	Prayed heartfelt prayers in private (Mark 1:35)	So he could have a flourishing personal relationship with the Father (Matt 6:6)
GIVING	Tithed extensively (Matt 23:23)	So people could see their generosity (Matt 6:2)	Gave his life (John 10:18)	So all who would believe in Jesus may not die in their sin but have eternal life (John 3:16)
FASTING	Fasted and took on the appearance of one fasting (Matt 6:16)	So people would see the secret and intimate prayers between them and God (Matt 6:16)	Fasted for 40 days in the desert, where no-one could see (Matt 4:2)	So people did not know the secret and intimate prayers between Him and God (Matt 6:6)

TABLE 1: JESUS' OBEDIENCE VS. THE
PHARISEES' OBEDIENCE

the religious believe they can achieve salvation without it.

RIGHTEOUS OBEDIENCE: THE SPIRIT

Spirit-filled people obey God because they love God. They recognize that God is worthy of obedience and so they want to follow his commandments. They perform righteous actions with a righteous heart. How do you know where your heart is?

It's extremely difficult to know the state of our hearts. On the one hand, the heart is the wellspring of life; it births the desires and motives behind our actions (Proverbs 4:23). However, the heart is also deceitful, pulling us to commit terrible sin (Jeremiah 17:9). If we are to be righteous, we must recognize that our hearts are rudders that are capable of anything – good or evil. Therefore, we must plead with God to create new hearts within us, as David did:

> Create in me a pure heart, O God, and renew a steadfast spirit within me. Do not cast me from your presence or take your Holy Spirit from me. Restore to me the joy of your salvation and grant me a willing spirit, to sustain me – (Psalm 51:10–12).

A righteous person obeys God regardless of who is watching; when it is easy and when it is difficult, because they know that obedience leads to joy. Lots of people think joy and happiness mean the same thing. They're wrong. God wants to give you the former, he isn't so fussed about providing the latter. As you read the New Testament, you'll slowly realize that the early Church was full of courage. In Acts 4, the church rejoices when Peter and John are arrested. In Acts 16, Paul and Silas get thrown in prison and start singing hymns. James 1:2–3 says we should have joy in times of tribulation. Surely these men were insane? You arrest me, I'll be looking for revenge. You imprison me, I'll start planning the sequel to The Shawshank Redemption. When I'm going through trials, the last thing I feel is positive. Who would want to celebrate the jagged edges of life? That's ridiculous.

Not for the Christian. Happiness is a transient emotion. It ebbs and flows like the tide. I could start my day happy and then a stubbed toe, parking ticket or rude email later, and my account is empty. If happiness is so easily robbed, why does everyone pursue it so much?

Joy is unbreakable inner peace. How do you hear 'it's cancer' without the bottom falling out of your world? What about 'you're fired', or 'it's over'? What keeps you afloat when the ship is sinking? Joy.

As the coronavirus pandemic showed the world, everything in life can be taken from you in an instant. Nearly 1.44 million people have died worldwide. Unemployment in the UK rose from 3.8 per cent to 4.8 per cent. The International Monetary Fund said COVID-19 caused the worst global economic decline since the Great Depression of the 1930s[34]. Your money can be stolen, your body can become diseased and your friends and family will die. We find happiness in the temporary: our hobbies, jobs, bank accounts, health, relationships, achievements, etc. When these things are taken from us, happiness goes out the window. Joy is knowing that God has got you regardless of your circumstances. When you can't pay your rent, take heart, because God has not left you. When you're made redundant remember that they may take your job but they can never take away your God.

Joy does not make you impervious to pain – joy means you are not utterly devastated by the difficulties that life will throw at you. Anyone can be happy when everything is going well. It takes joy to stand up when life knocks you down. Happiness is lost in a second. Joy will always sustain you. We obey God because God knows all and wants us to experience life to the full. Joy, not necessarily happiness, is God's destination for our obedience. He does not want to ruin our lives but wants us to have the best lives possible.

GETHSEMANE: OBEDIENCE OF A SPIRIT-FILLED MAN

> Jesus went out as usual to the Mount of Olives, and his disciples followed him. On reaching the place, he said to them, 'Pray that you will not fall into temptation.' He withdrew about a stone's throw beyond them, knelt down and prayed, 'Father, if you are willing, take this cup from me; yet not my will, but yours be done.' An angel from heaven appeared to him and strengthened him. And being in anguish, he prayed more earnestly, and his sweat was like drops of blood falling down to the ground – (Luke 22:39–44).

In the garden of Gethsemane, Jesus decided to obey the hardest command that would ever be given to a human being: to die for the sin of humankind. It's important to realize the difference between Jesus' death and every other death. Jesus is a part of the Trinity: three persons of God that are one, who have been in communion for eternity. However, when Jesus died, that relationship was momentarily severed, and the Father crushed the Son. An infinite, unfettered, joy-filled communion of love was broken in Jesus' death, as he carried the weight of our sin.

Here's an example to push the point home: Imagine you knew your partner was going to die. Horrifying, right? Now imagine you had the choice to either let your spouse die to save someone else's life or let your spouse live while the other person dies. I know for the more selfless ones among you, this may be a bit of a dilemma. For me, this is easy: I'm choosing Clare. Let's take this analogy further: imagine being given the choice to sacrifice your spouse to save this other person's life? Moreover, imagine the person whose life you were going to save was malicious and spiteful towards you and your spouse: spitting at you whenever they saw you; breaking into your home and throwing stones at you. Scandalous, isn't it? Why would anyone want to help such a degenerate?

This is the choice that God made. God the Father chose to pick up the blade, and God the Son chose to remain on the table. His Father, the one he had known so intimately for so long, plunged the blade into his chest.

That is obedience.

Jesus did not want the cross. He wanted another way, something that wouldn't be as brutal. Something that wouldn't break his most treasured relationship. Something that wouldn't have his Father nail him to a tree. Yet, Jesus put his wants aside and chose obedience. He submitted to the Father's wish and was executed on the cross. He took upon himself the weight of all our sin, past, present and future. He died and was raised to life, paying sin's price and offering us forgiveness. An act of such obedience that no Christian will ever have to endure again. And so, when we obey God, we look to Jesus as our standard.

Obedience is not easy.

Obedience may shake us to the point of sweating blood, just like Jesus. Obedience may not end well for us. Obedience to God could mean our own death. Obedience however, is our submission to God, where we say: not our will but your will be done. People filled with the Spirit of God are obedient people.

> The one who keeps God's commands lives in him, and
> he in him. And this is how we know that he lives in us:
> we known it by the Spirit he gave us – (1 John 3:24).

STOP & THINK

People that abide in the Spirit of God harness the power to obey God's commands joyfully because they love God. People that do not abide in the Spirit of God obey God's commands religiously because they want to earn God's favour. So, take a look at the heart behind your actions. Spend a few minutes in silence, picturing Jesus in the garden of Gethsemane. Think about his obedience. Mull it over. Then, answer the following questions:

1. Do you obey God?
2. Why do you obey him?
3. Do you think God will punish you if you don't obey him?
4. Do you want to obey God's commandments?
5. Do you find some commandments easier to obey than others?
6. Do you ever do 'holy' things (eg pray, worship, Bible reading etc) so that others may compliment you on how holy you are?
7. What do you think of Jesus' decision in Gethsemane?

LOVE

ABIDE IN LOVE

8

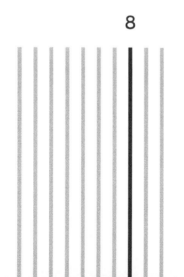

Beloved, let us love one another, for love is from God, and whoever loves has been born of God and knows God. Anyone who does not love does not know God, because God is love.

In this the love of God was made manifest among us, that God sent his only Son into the world, so that we might live through him.

In this is love, not that we have loved God but that he loved us and sent his Son to be the propitiation for our sins.

Beloved, if God so loved us, we also ought to love one another. No one has ever seen God; if we love one another, God abides in us and his love is perfected in us.

By this we know that we abide in him and he in us, because he has given us of his Spirit. And we have seen and testify that the Father has sent his Son to be the Saviour of the world. Whoever confesses that Jesus is the Son of God, God abides in him, and he in God.

1 John 4:7 - 15

We cannot define it, nor create it in a lab, yet everyone understands love. For life to be worth living, love is essential. Our songs are littered with love and our thoughts are consumed with love for our significant others, our families and our friends. Moreover, we all know love because we know the pain of loss.

Let me explain my point with a bunch of spoilers. If you haven't seen *The Lion King, The Fault in Our Stars* nor *Titanic*, repent...and skip the rest of this paragraph. Did we not all weep when Mufasa died saving Simba's life? Who cannot recall the tears and snot when I just mention the word 'Gus'? For you oldies, weren't you an absolute mess when Rose finally let Jack go? [35]

Breaking up with partners, the loss of a pet, watching friends move away or losing loved ones through estrangement, conflict or even death are devastating events. Love is not a feeling; love is a currency.

The Bible not only acknowledges this but ups the ante – it commands us to love. The greatest commandment is to love God and the second is to love your neighbour as yourself (Mark 12:28-31). I think about myself a lot: my needs, my wants, my failures, my dreams, my schedule etc. For me to give another person the same attention is an intimidating task. Modern psychology says that our capacity to love comes from the amount of love we have been shown. I am fortunate enough to have had two loving parents, a relatively pleasant family and plenty of considerate friends. I've been loved more than most and yet I feel I do not have the capacity to love others as I love me. I try and give others the attention and affection that I offer myself and it works...for three days. Then your nose-picking, chew-with-your-mouth-open and skid marks-in-the-toilet-bowl hygiene is too much. If love is a currency, people drive me to bankruptcy.

Are you like me? Do you struggle with loving people as much as you love yourself? This chapter will look at how love is the foundation upon which the entire Christian faith is built. We will plunge into God's scandalous love and look at how abiding in such love leads us out of fear and into freedom.

GOD'S LOVE

Our ability to love is based on recognizing the overwhelming amount of love we have received from God.

> This is love: not that we have loved God, but that he loved us and sent his Son as an atoning sacrifice for our sins. –(1 John 4:10).

Let's break this verse down into three key ideas: The Father sent: 'He loved us and sent…'; His beloved Son: 'his Son as an atoning sacrifice'; For his enemies: 'Not that we loved have God…'.

THE FATHER SENT

God first loved Adam and Eve, creating and granting them dominion, happiness and purpose within the Garden of Eden. Eating the apple proved that their love was more like treason, yet he mercifully spared their lives, declaring that they were to give rise to the seed (Jesus) who would crush the head of Satan – the tempter who had goaded them into disobeying God[36]. Abraham's fear took him to the point that he sold his own wife into slavery, yet God continued to love him despite his sin and he became the father of the Jewish faith[37]. Speaking of Jews, the whole Old Testament is a broken record: Israel sins, God sends a prophet and Israel repents[38]. Repeat ten or eleven times. Sin, prophet, repent. Sin, prophet, repent. The funny thing is, God gave Israel a sacrificial system (the Law) by which they could be forgiven[39] before the broken record was ever played.

Fast forward 400 years and Jesus arrived – the perfect example of mercy and grace. Jesus undertook the sacrifice that eclipsed all sacrifices – for his death covered all sin: past, present and future. What Jesus did is proof that God first loved us. I used to sing this catchy song called 'I've found Jesus' – but that title is fundamentally incorrect; Jesus has been coming after us since before Eden.

HIS BELOVED SON

Have you ever stopped to watch children play with their parents at the park? Don't get caught gazing because you may get landed with a restraining order but, provided you keep a low profile, you can catch moments of magic between the tantrums and the feeds. I can see it now. The kid struggles to clamber up the ladder and mum gives her a push. With absolutely no grace but the cuteness of a kitten, she wanders to the slide, looks mummy dead in the eye and musters up the courage to go down all by herself. There's the inevitable 'Weeeeee!' and, as mummy scoops up her little, overdressed-for-autumn bundle of gold, the toddler exclaims, 'I love you mummy!' and she whispers the same back. Wiping the glint in his eye, dad captures the whole thing on film. Meanwhile, you're watching this episode from a behind a nearby tree blowing your nose and wiping your own eyes with a Kleenex.

Yes, it's a little cheesy but these moments often are. There's something beautifully ferocious about the love between a parent and child. It's a fine balance between 'Come and see my amazing kid' to 'Harm a hair on their head and they'll never find your body'. Isn't this why so many of us are so scared to pick up our friends' babies? It's not the injury the baby will incur if we were to drop it; it's the fact that momma has a tombstone ready for anyone who does. It's lovely, but almost scary, how much a parent loves their child.

Take that ferocious love, times it by a billion, carry the one and you've got a slice of the love within the Trinity. The relationship between Jesus, the Father and the Holy Spirit is unlike anything on earth. Jesus came from heaven, which means he was with God, as a part of God, from eternity past. The Father loved the Son, who loved the Spirit, who loved the Father, who loved the Son, who loved the Spirit, so on and so forth. An intricate weaving of infinite beings that laughed, celebrated and encouraged one another for an eternity. I can just imagine some of their conversations:

'Great work on finishing the Milky Way, Holy Spirit.'

'Thanks, I love what we did with the Great Barrier Reef. Jesus, do you need help with the edges of the universe?'

Countless moments of quality time spent in perfect harmony as the Father loves the Son who loves the Spirit, so on and so forth.

Sex is the union of two bodies, two minds and two souls. It is the greatest single act of intimacy we can conceive. The intimacy in the Trinity makes sex look like a handshake. Our earthly relations compared to heaven look sad and superficial. Jesus had a perfect relationship with the Father, yet he left paradise to come and rescue us. He left the magic-slide-moments and the daily embrace of the infinite ones to live as an impoverished Palestinian.

When Adam and Eve sinned in the garden, God sacrificed an animal to give them skins to cover their shame (Genesis 3:21). When a Jew sinned, they had to slaughter cattle, sheep, goats, birds or rams to atone for their sin[40]. God always provides a way for sinners to be forgiven. The way never changes. The way always works. The way is sacrifice. You do wrong, something innocent must bleed.

It was our sins that did that to him, that ripped and tore

and crushed him—our sins! He took the punishment,
and that made us whole. Through his bruises we get
healed. We're all like sheep who've wandered off and
gotten lost. We've all done our own thing, gone our
own way. And GOD has piled all our sins, everything
we've done wrong, on him, on him – (Isaiah 53:5–6,
The Message).

All the sacrifices in the Old Testament point to the greatest sacrifice in
history. Yes, Jesus died to take all our sins away but what we forget is
that a father lost a son. No, it's worse than that; a father's son was killed.
The nails went through his hands and feet because of our wrongdoing.
He was the true Passover lamb whose blood spared us from the wrath
of God (Exodus 12:7). On the cross, Jesus died a thousand deaths. Lest
we forget, as his son hung on the cross, the Father cried a thousand
tears. Which of us would be that gracious? Which of us would be that
reckless? Our sin did not just tear Jesus apart; it tore his family apart.

FOR HIS ENEMIES

Since we read the Bible retrospectively, Jesus always looks like the good
guy. We scold the crowd that releases Barabbas (Matthew 27:11–26),
but forget that, at the height of Jesus' fame, he had become a polarizing
and dangerous figure. There was team Jesus – a small group of misfits –
and team anti-Jesus – the ruling power brokers in Jerusalem. Jesus had
amassed quite a following but also had several unsavoury encounters
with the Pharisees. His reputation grew with every passing miracle
and things escalated to the point that his opponents viewed him as
a political threat who would completely change the status quo (John
11:50). He dined with social outcasts: tax collectors, prostitutes and
lepers (Mark 2:15). Some of the Pharisees even started to defect to
Jesus' side. So they decided: he had to go. His opponents managed to
convince the occupying Roman force that Jesus would become a serious

threat to Caesar. Since Rome hated revolts, they were more than happy to oblige. It didn't take much to twist Pontius Pilate's arm and have Jesus killed. Matthew recorded a conversation between Jesus and the executioners just before they marched him to death. Read this slowly and put yourself in the scene. Be the fly on the wall as we look more closely at the day of Jesus' death, the day we still call 'Good Friday'.

> Then the governor's soldiers took Jesus into the Praetorium and gathered the whole company of soldiers round him. They stripped him and put a scarlet robe on him, and then twisted together a crown of thorns and set it on his head. They put a staff in his right hand. Then they knelt in front of him and mocked him. 'Hail, king of the Jews!' they said. They spat on him, and took the staff and struck him on the head again and again. After they had mocked him, they took off the robe and put his own clothes on him. Then they led him away to crucify him – (Matthew 27:27–31).

They wedged a crown of thorns on his head. They beat him as they taunted him. They stripped him naked in front of eighty men and knelt before him in jest. Consider the irony: the man they mock as king, is the King of Kings[41]. They crowned him with thorns, completely unaware that they didn't even deserve to be in his presence. They struck him as if he was a helpless dog, yet they didn't know the most powerful being in the universe was reeling at the end of their rod. They disgraced the one who at that exact point in time was performing the most gracious act in history.

To really force the point home, think about this: Jesus created all things out of the overflow of his words (John 1:1–4). He crafted every human from the dust of the earth and breathed life into their lungs. He has been at work in the womb of every woman who has given birth, including those who gave birth to these very soldiers. Jesus knew these spiteful men not just by name, but by nature. He moulded their DNA, saw their first steps, chuckled the first time they asked a girl out and listened to their fears during their first tours as Roman soldiers. But here, he recoiled at the end of their fists. As they forced spines onto his head, struck his back with clubs and spit in his face, temptation must have started to stir in the Nazarene's mind: 'Why don't I click my fingers and erase them from history? I could call down a legion of angels to dash them to pieces?' He chose to stay silent.

It took three of them to heap the cross-bar onto his back. Marching through the streets, they led him up a hill to the local dump, whipping him every time he fell. The cackles echoed as the bloodthirsty mob piled on the insults and threw rotting food at the procession – news must've spread fast. Then they arrived. Golgotha looked like a derelict landfill. It would have stunk, littered as it was with the remains of blood and faeces from previously executed prisoners. Throwing him to the ground, they took the cross-bar and tied it to the vertical plank on the floor. His screams pierced as they jammed tetanus-infected spikes through his wrists, sending a sensation up his arm that would've felt like electrified fire. They erected his bloodied and broken excuse of a body for all to see.

Can you picture it? Can you see the ghastly figure of God? Can you hear his agony? Can you see the soldiers' delight? Where are you in this whole ordeal? You may feel that you are Jesus' mother Mary, weeping alongside John as they murder your dearly loved son and saviour. You may feel like Jesus' disciples: scared, alone and abandoned. However, Romans 5:8 says that: 'While we were still sinners, Christ died for us'. Before God changed our lives, we didn't believe him, we didn't love him and we certainly weren't on his side.

Therefore, I think that if you were in Jerusalem at the time, you wouldn't have been a fan of Jesus: too controversial and too extreme. So, are you the crowd, who are baying for Jesus' blood? No. I believe it's worse. You and I are the soldiers. We mock the king, who is the King of Kings. We did not come to God as Jews came to sacrifice. We did not come to God, pleading that he accept our bull. God came to us, and we dismissed him as just another joke. Our sin is spit in his face. 'Live like this? Act like this? Pray like this? Worship you? Hahaha. Get out of my face, you backward, Nazarene peasant. Better yet Pilate, crucify him. Let's be done with this circus already.' The voice God gave me to worship, I used to curse his name. The fingers God gave me to cultivate his beautiful planet, I used for my own pursuits. I may as well have put the nails through his hands myself. That's what it means to be an enemy of God.

To a human eye, the people who were in attendance were Jesus' mother, the soldiers, the mob, the two criminals being crucified alongside him and his frightened followers. However, there are two more. Can you see their tears? Can you feel their sorrow? The Son bleeds from Roman timber as the Father and the Spirit do nothing but watch. Can you imagine the blend of anger, grief and torment they would have felt as they gazed upon their beloved?

Gods don't die. That's the chief pre-requisite to being a god – invincibility. Our God chose to do what no god has ever done. And for what? Remorseful sinners who approach the throne with their tails between their legs? No. God died for a bunch of stupid, ignorant soldiers. When God died for you, you were not his friend. Neither were you on neutral terms. While you were his enemy, God died for you.

WHAT DOES GOD'S LOVE MEAN?

At your worst, God died for you. It wasn't when you realized that sin was even a thing, but way before then. Abiding in love is knowing that

God could not love us anymore and will not love us any less. If he sent his beloved Son to be killed for your mistakes, while you were making your mistakes, your debt is paid!

> God made him who had no sin to be sin for us, so that in him we might become the righteousness of God – (2 Corinthians 5:21).

Theologians call this 'The Great Exchange': Jesus takes our sin, we take Jesus' righteousness. We clothed him in filth, and he clothed us in gold. It's the greatest transaction of all time. But, here's the climax: Jesus rose again. Sin did not destroy him, nor could death hold him. He rose from the ashes, victorious over it all. After three days away from his family, Jesus' resurrection proves that our sin has been dealt with forever. This is why 'Gospel' means 'good news'. He did it! He lived the life we should have lived and died the death we should have died. But why?

Love.

Not just love for the Father or the Spirit but love for you. He died to show you, his enemy, that God is willing to go to hell and back just to have you.

God's love is not just a feeling; it's the foundation of our faith. He created us out of love and left heaven because of love. Love put him to death and his love put death to death. His love for his children is fearfully huge, yet his love casts fear out of all his children. He does not sprinkle us with his love, nor throw out an 'I love you' with a card and flowers. He drenches us in love, saturating us underneath the waterfall and then boots us out that we may drip it everywhere we go. To a friend, we say 'Come and meet my Father' and to a foe, we say 'Father, forgive them, they have no idea what they're missing out on.' God's love is indescribable, insurmountable and unrivalled. If love is a currency, we have been given keys to the treasury. We shall never be bankrupt again.

STOP & THINK

John says 'This is how God showed his love among us' (1 John 4:9). Unlike our vague and undefinable concept of love, God's love is obvious. It's the death and resurrection of his beloved Son, who promises eternal life to all who believe in him, period. Everything hinges on that. And so, you have a choice. God has made the first move, and now the ball is in your court. Are you going to abide in the love of God, or not? Read the previous paragraph slowly. Let it sink in. Read it a third time if you need to. Now, once you're aware of the scandalously huge love of God, take the time to honestly answer the following questions:

1. Do you think God loves you?
2. Do you struggle to accept God's love?
3. Do you think you could earn God's love?
4. Are you afraid of God?
5. Do you love yourself?
6. How well have you loved others around you?

FREEDOM

ABIDE IN PEACE

9

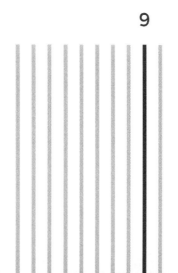

So we have come to know and to believe the love that God has for us. God is love, and whoever abides in love abides in God, and God abides in him.

By this is love perfected with us, so that we may have confidence for the day of judgment, because as he is so also are we in this world.

There is no fear in love, but perfect love casts out fear. For fear has to do with punishment, and whoever fears has not been perfected in love. We love because he first loved us. If anyone says, "I love God," and hates his brother, he is a liar; for he who does not love his brother whom he has seen cannot love God whom he has not seen.

And this commandment we have from him: whoever loves God must also love his brother.

1 John 4:15-21

The Gospel changes everything. It is not mere information, but truth that transforms. There are so many uses for the Gospel in your life but, in this chapter, John focuses on one specific application – freedom – in three specific areas:

1.   Freedom from fear.
2.   Freedom to love yourself.
3.   Freedom to love others.

FREE FROM FEAR

The Bible clearly outlines the holiness of God. Conversely, it also goes into great depth to describe the un-holiness of humanity. Every time God sets the bar, we fall short. Therefore, the Bible is filled with many instances where God judged unrighteous people. Sodom and Gomorrah was burned to the ground (Genesis 19). God flooded the entire earth, killing everyone but one family and a small zoo (Genesis 6–9). God's people were conquered by foreign kingdoms and cast into exile, twice[42]. We should be scared of God for we have no excuse; sinners must pay the price of sin.

The religious understand this well. The basic principle to religion is simple: do certain acts to pay for your sin. Sacrifice this lamb; pray this prayer; do x, y or z first, then God will be pleased with you. Religion doesn't even have to be centred in a particular faith. You can be a perfectly religious atheist, or spiritualist. Perhaps your acts may be reflection, meditating, yoga or whatever it is to get your mind 'right'. Nonetheless, there's a fundamental problem with religion: how do you know when enough is enough? How many 'Hail Marys' does it take to atone for the drugs I took last night? How many pilgrimages to Mecca will compensate for my fits of rage? How long will I have to practice mindfulness to excuse my need to control?

Because of this unfortunate truth, at the core of a religious person is fear. This isn't a healthy reverence of God, this is a chills-down-the-spine, waking-up-in-a-cold-sweat sort of fear. John uses the word 'phobos', from which we get our word phobia, to describe it (1 John 4:18). Religious people should be scared, because they never know what kind of God they shall meet in the great beyond. So many are extremely pious and constantly worried about putting a foot wrong lest they burn in hell. Others try, but cannot pray five times a day, keep forgetting the words of the Lord's Prayer and fall asleep every time they meditate. They despair for they know the only thing that awaits them is hell. The Gospel frees us from the fear of religion.

Religion says that you must pay God back, then God will be happy with you. The Gospel says that God paid your debt, so God is happy with you. Because the Son was judged in our place, there's no condemnation for those who abide in Christ (Romans 8:1)! The Gospel frees its believers from God-phobia. I gave Jesus all my sin; Jesus gave me all his righteousness. All our debts have been paid.

However, we are forgetful and dumb. We often overlook God's grace and start to fear God's punishment, especially when we sin. Paul wrestled with his sin like the rest of us do:

> What a wretched man I am! Who will rescue me from this body that is subject to death? Thanks be to God, who delivers me through Jesus Christ our Lord! – (Romans 7:24–25a).

In our own struggles, we must remind ourselves that we should fear God, but not be afraid of God. We do need to recognize that we resist his commands and miss his standards of holiness.

Anger. Arrogance. Doubt. Jealously. Lying. Lust. Piracy. Porn. Pride.

Religion. Self-centredness. Work-a-holism. These sins have plagued me most of my life. They fight me in the morning and sometimes keep me up at night. Some have taken me to therapy. Some are still life-controlling. Sometimes I have good days; sometimes I don't.

In addition to my sin, I have to fight the religious monkey on my back. It goes something like this. Let's say I think of a smutty video or lewd clip I've seen or I say something spiteful to Clare, or think that I'm more holy, cool, or intelligent than the people around me. It's not great, I repent, and try to move on. But for whatever reason my lust, my anger and my pride won't let me go. Three days later, I'm thinking of another video, biting someone else's head off or perfecting my social media just right so that everybody can see just how holy, cool or intelligent I am. Again, it's not great, I repent…again, and try to move on. The problem is, this time I'm not so quick to do so. There's a bit less energy, a bit less gusto, a bit less momentum because there's a bit less faith that I'll ever be able to shake the darker side of me.

This is where religion comes in. Here I am trying to fill my mind with good things to erase the smut in my mind's movie screen, the fire from my mouth and pop the hot air in my metaphorical massive head. I'm praying, journaling and on occasion texting Jon Brown (my best mate) in an effort to overcome. If that's not hard enough, another line of thought wanders in:

> Why would God love me? I'm terrible. I can't go to church like this, I'm a leader. I should probably pray more. I should probably read a few more chapters this morning. I can't just…come as I am, I'm filthy.

Do you see how religious that is? It's so tempting to try and clean myself up before coming to God for forgiveness, as if that was even possible. I'm learning to realize that God loved me when I was a lustful, angry and self-absorbed narcissist. He saw me at my worst, and still went to the cross. Moreover, it's not just religious, it's arrogant to try and clean myself up before God will accept me. Religion has the audacity to say 'Don't worry God, I've got this. You don't need to die on the cross, my sacrifice will do.' The whole reason Jesus died is because we are not clean, nor can we make ourselves clean. There weren't enough religious acts that would pay my debt, nor did I want to do any of them. So, God did.

Realizing the power of the gospel has set me free to love him. I can run to him. I can bring my mind, my mouth and my ego to the Father. I can take solace in knowing that he can and does help me in my time of need. He does not hate me, so I approach the throne of God with all my mess. God does not love us more on our 'good days' and less on 'bad days'. God's perfect love casts out fear. What is there to be scared of? The word 'perfect' in 1 John 4:18 means 'complete'. In other words, God's love is completed when someone receives and harnesses its true power: the power to bring both the pervert and the pious man to the foot of the cross.

Therefore, the mark that you have been changed by the Gospel is that you run to God when you screw up, instead of running away from him. That is what it means for God's love to be perfected in you. I'm not there yet, but I'm so thankful that I'm learning to run there more often.

FREE TO LOVE YOURSELF

Strike the right pose. Use the correct filter. Look your best and hide your flaws. Social media has distilled this down to an artform. It's now common sport to get the most followers or acquire the most subscriptions. How do you do that? Present the beautiful and hide the ugly. That's what the world wants. Make your Instagram a highlight reel, not the whole reel. When's the last time someone tweeted: 'The last three days have been ordinary. I went to work, did some shopping and made some spaghetti?' Someone may have tweeted that, but I can bet they've been at fourteen followers for three years now (and at least half are family). Here's the problem with that mindset: shame. Putting your best foot forward means there's still a foot behind. To every good side, there's a repulsive one. Better yet, to every edited image, there's an original. For all our boasting about being authentic, the last thing our culture does is keep it real.

The result is a vicious cycle of comparison and shame. Living like this is a lose-lose. On the one hand, if you can keep up the charade, you've entered a life of constant comparison.

> She looks like this, so I'm going to have to look better. Snap. Edit. Post. Likes. They look like they're having a vibe, so I'm going to have to turn this soggy lasagne into a Pinterest dinner party. Snap. Edit. Post. More likes. Now all I got to do is maintain my size zero and sell a kidney to keep funding this thing.

You don't go to parties anymore to enjoy them; you go to get snaps with the in-crowd. The beach is not for sunbathing, but to take bikini shots. Sunsets aren't for gazing; they are for providing amazing light so you can brag with #nofilter. You'll have followers and fans, but you'll be running the hamster wheel of doing things you don't want to please people you don't like, all in the hope of someone loving a slice of you – the side you work so hard to craft.

On the other hand, most people aren't able to do that. Most of us don't have thousands of subscribers or a mailing list. Most of us are fat (or think we are), un-photogenic (or just ugly), geeky (not in the Elon Musk way, but the Microsoft-Excel-spreadsheet way), out of shape or just plain boring. Everyone laughed at our nudes, our Tik Toks were awful and the furthest we've been on holiday is Tesco. We cannot keep up with the hamster wheel. We can't keep up the façade and so we're left with this inescapable feeling that we are the problem. It's not the system, it's us.

Shame.

There it is again.

The scientists agree. A 2017 survey of 1,479 young people had some startling findings[43]:

- Ninety-one per cent of sixteen to twenty-four-year olds use social media.
- Social media has been described as more addictive than cigarettes and alcohol.
- Rates of anxiety and depression in young people have risen seventy per cent in the past twenty-five years.
- Social media use is linked with increased rates of anxiety, depression and poor sleep.
- Nine out of ten girls are unhappy with their body.
- Ninety-one per cent of users have experienced cyberbullying.

Culture says hide your flaws, so we keep trying and failing, getting up, trying and failing again. In the end the cycle leaves us depressed, on edge and, most of all, exhausted. Sounds like falling off the hamster wheel to me.

However, there are some immensely helpful people out there who have noticed this trend of shame and encouraged people to take off the mask. The LGBTQ community used to be shunned, mocked, picketed, bullied and even prosecuted. Alan Turing[44], the guy responsible for cracking coded Nazi messages and helping the Allies win the Second World War, was convicted of 'indecency' (ie homosexuality) seven years after the war ended. For centuries, black people in the West were seen as sub-human. Women have been on the battered side of history for millennia. Black Panther is the direct result of Martin Luther King Jr, the chief of the black civil rights movement. #MeToo is a direct result of Emily Pankhurst, the figurehead of the feminist movement. Pride is a direct result of Harvey Milk, the gay-rights advocate.

Whether you agree with their movements or not, the fantastic thrust of these movements is that they say no with a strong exclamation point. They rally and they march because they are free of the shame that society places upon them. They are free of culture dictating to them what filter they should use, what dress size they should squeeze into or what sexual orientation they should follow. They wear their hair naturally, dress in the clothes of the opposite gender or burn their bras. Screw the hamster wheel, they make it OK for you to be you. They encourage you to take your mask off, rather than keep up the farce.

It's unbelievably freeing, but, sadly, this freedom doesn't go far enough. Gay people, you should be ashamed. Black people, you should be ashamed. Women, you should be ashamed. To all the marginalized minorities, the Gospel says with its own exclamation: you should be ashamed! For all the times your words cut others down, the lies, tantrums of anger, adultery, violence and all the other mess that keeps your conscience up at night. Being a victim does not excuse you from the sins that are common to all humankind. God still had to die. Just because you are a black feminist lesbian doesn't mean you were not there. You were right next to me as we put nails into the hands of God.

The Gospel forces a person to look at their true self. Nothing else will show us the depth of our disgrace more clearly than the death of Jesus. However, nothing else will show us the titanic heights of our worth more clearly than the death of Jesus. The Gospel shows us that while we were despicable, we are worth it. It raises sinners from the ashes and lets them fly. The Gospel doesn't just free us from the shame of culture; it frees us from the shame we place upon ourselves. It looks at our flaws and covers them in his blood.

This is true freedom. This is why a Christian can throw off their shame, because God crushed it. He is the only one who saw the full depth of your depravity and didn't turn away.

So when it comes to loving yourself, culture says hide your ugly side and love the side you show the world. The activists say you have no ugly side, and so love yourself warts and all. The Gospel says you have an ugly side, and God made it beautiful. Free from your shame, you can truly love yourself.

FREE TO LOVE OTHERS

If we let the overwhelming love of God permeate our heads and hearts, we are given the supernatural capacity to love other people. Let's start with the head. All people were made by God, for God. The postman, your mates at work and your family. Their original, ideal and proper place in the universe is within the bosom of God. Unfortunately, the primary problem with the human condition is that we are, by default, far from God. Therefore, the most loving thing that someone can do for someone else is not to help them stop smoking, improve their educational outcomes or help with their failing marriage, it's to push them closer to God.

This should fuel our heart's desire to see people who are far from God encounter God for themselves. For too long the Christian faith has been about spreading the Gospel to save people from hell. This reduces the Gospel to a simple get-out-of-hell-free card. We do not believe in

Jesus to avoid hell; we believe in Jesus because we love God. He is our goal and our great reward. You may have a roof over your head, money in your pocket and a lover on your arm, but, without Jesus, you've only smelled the appetiser. The mantra that should constantly be on a Christian's lips is, 'I was where you were, but trust me: Jesus is better.'

That's an easy message to share with people you love, right? It's not hard to share the most important thing in your life to people that love you. How often do you hear about people's love for their kids, Call of Duty or their spouses? Beyoncé has pretty much started a cult. Ivy Park. Trolling Becky with the Good Hair. The fact that everyone knows how to dance when 'Crazy in love' comes on. Forget WWJD, Yoncé fans are the best evangelists I know. It's natural to share your heart with those you are close to, and so it should be with us. We should be people that sacrifice our money, time and talent to see people far from God transformed by the power of the Gospel. Therefore, please don't see evangelism as inviting someone to church or standing on a soapbox and declaring hell in the town square. Get to know your friends, neighbours and co-workers. What makes them tick? What do they struggle with? How can you love them better? How can you serve them? They are not projects to be completed but people to be loved. Once you build a heart-to-heart connection with someone, you'll see what's most important to them, and they'll see what's most important to you. It's at that junction that the Gospel is seen not just by your words, but by your actions of love. But, that's not freedom. It's loving, but not freedom.

As Jesus hung on the cross, he muttered something very peculiar, 'Father, forgive them, for they do not know what they are doing' (Luke 23:34). With his dying breath, he wanted us to be closer to God because he knew that was best for us. Why didn't he want to kill us? Why didn't he want to get his own back?

The Gospel frees a person from revenge and grants them the power of compassion. When someone harms us, our response is to get even: an eye for an eye and a tooth for a tooth. That's justice, right? That's the way the world works, and it suits us just fine. So why didn't Jesus demand justice? Why did he choose suffering? He wanted his enemies to experience the love of God. Jesus' desire for people to know the love of God extended beyond the borders of people that he liked. As he bled, he felt compassion. Between the screams of pain, He felt sadness – a sobering pity that all these scoffers, soldiers and hypocritical religious people were so far from the love of God. They thought they were doing the right thing in killing him, but it was actually the most stupid decision in history.

How are you able to have such stability in such chaos? How do you go through the most bitter of trials and not be torn apart? You harness the overwhelming love of God. True freedom is saying that, regardless of your response to me, I will show you the love of God. I will serve you, as you strike me. I will show you the other cheek, walk the second mile and refuse to take justice by force; rather I will show mercy and grace.

STOP & THINK

Knowing God's love makes me feel so wonderful about myself. I haven't got to perform; I haven't got to achieve – I can just breathe. Moreover, if God makes me feel like this, I wonder if this medicine could work on others. You see it's his effect on me that makes me want to talk about him. However, I don't know if I have the strength to pray and bless those who would hurt me. As I write, a black man called George Floyd is the latest racist killing in a long line of African-American murders in the last few years. He was killed by suffocation by former police officer Derek Chauvin. Derek knelt on George's his neck for almost nine minutes all because he was under suspicion of using a counterfeit twenty dollar bill in a nearby store.

Freedom means loving murderers by forgiving and blessing them. I don't have that sense of compassion, yet. Jesus did. True freedom means loving people despite what they do to you. It's unbelievable, damn near unachievable, but such a beautiful concept that Jesus modelled wonderfully on the cross. Where do we get that kind of inner strength? Where do we get that stability? We harness the overwhelming love of God. Here's how I think we can do that.

Put yourself back in the scene of the crucifixion. Jesus is naked, bleeding, abandoned and dying. As you stare, his teary eyes scan the scene. He's not got long. The watchers are laughing, crying and mocking. His friends are nowhere to be seen and Mary is blended into the crowds at the back. She is a mess. His eyes meet yours for a second and he says, 'Father, forgive them, for they do not know what they are doing.'

How do you feel?

For me, I'm happy, sad and inspired. I still cannot believe it. He knew he would rise again. He knew he'd be abandoned by God and kin. Yet he still went through with it. All to have me. To have us! How beautiful. How formidable. I also see an example that can change the world. I see a man who inspired other men to fight fire with love. I see a lion, as well as a lamb. Both free. He didn't care what his enemies did, but used God's love to walk all the way to death. Where else could I find such freedom?

What do you see?

EPILOGUE

ABIDE IN THE SON

10

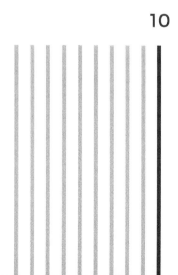

And this is the testimony, that God gave us eternal life, and this life is in his Son. Whoever has the Son has life; whoever does not have the Son of God does not have life.

I write these things to you who believe in the name of the Son of God that you may know that you have eternal life. And this is the confidence that we have toward him, that if we ask anything according to his will he hears us.

1 John 5:11-14

One would think that after twenty-six years of walking, I'd have it down. Apparently not. A few years ago, I was taken to Mount Snowdon in Gwynedd, Wales. For those of you that have never visited, it's one of the most picturesque places in the UK, attracting several million visitors per year. Set amongst the Snowdonia national park, the mount is the highest peak south of the Scottish Highlands, offering gorgeous views of the undulating hills and valleys. On a good day, you can even see Ireland.

I had been up Snowdon many times prior to this showdown, so I was brimming with excitement on the drive west with my colleagues from school. Getting to the top of Snowdon isn't difficult. There's an easy-to-navigate path that winds all the way to the peak, where you can put your feet up and bathe in the warmth of accomplishing 10,000 steps. There's even a visitor centre at the summit, sporting excellent tea and an overpriced gift shop. You have all the time in the world to let the sweat evaporate and the heart rate equalize as you grab the novelty pencils with your left while holding an English Breakfast in the right.

However, Neil and James had other plans. 'Yeah Neil, we'll do Crib Goch[45]. It's a lovely day,' James said across the breakfast table. I thought nothing of it. To be honest, I should've thought something was awry when I saw James pack rope into his backpack.

Crib Goch is a narrow ridge that forms part of an alternative route to the top known as the Snowdon Horseshoe. Clambering up the steep hills, I started to notice that this was not going to be like any of my previous trips to west Wales.

One: I was tired. The usual path has a shallow gradient, but this felt like climbing three steps at a time, all the time. My bum was feeling the burn. Two: there were a few people. Walking up Snowdon is a stampede, but this was a queue. Moreover, this crowd seemed much fitter than the usual; clearly their bums could handle the burn. Seven hundred calories and one oxygen mask later, we arrived at the narrow ridge. Crib Goch is as welcoming as it is intimidating. The knife-edged assembly of large and small grey-brown stones form a razorback that could be happily at home on the back of Godzilla. However, the deep cyan of the sky and the warmth of the sun compelled us to continue and so, we began.

Around halfway, I came to a new set of realizations. Three: I wasn't walking, I was scrambling. Scrambling fits somewhere between walking on all fours, Zumba and squats. The thing is, you must scramble on Crib Goch. The ridge creates such a gust that if you were to stand up, it would only be a matter of time before you got blown off the edge. Four: I was scared. Knowing that one false move to the right or three to the left would plunge you to a horrible death brings a level of fear that is sobering. Climbers far more experienced than I have died doing this walk. Some people were so scared they just stopped and clung to the rocks beneath, literally hugging the mountain. Watching experienced and cool-headed mountaineers encourage and coax them to carry on was heart-warming, but it didn't take away that sense that this was not a joke. Five: I was having the time of my life. Something about pushing your body into mortal danger is exhilarating. As we ended with sore backs and clothes soaked in nervous sweat, Neil turned to me and said, 'Not too bad, eh?' Too prideful to show my ecstasy at being alive, I did what any man in my position would do when plunged way out of his depth...I looked back coolly and nodded.

> Enter through the narrow gate. For wide is the gate and broad is the way that leads to destruction, and many enter through it. But small is the gate and narrow the road that leads to life, and only a few find it – (Matthew 7:13–14).

The Christian life is like Crib Goch. It's a narrow path littered with traps, obstacles and enemies. Jesus plainly said that we enter by the narrow gate, and those who find it are few. It'll be tiring, fun, at times extremely scary but, most of all, worthwhile. Therefore, it can be tempting to become extremely religious and adopt an SAS mindset, relying on our white-knuckled zeal to walk this road.

The most devoted followers to religious law 2,000 years ago were known as Pharisees. Not only did they give up to a quarter of all their money, assets and food to the synagogue, they memorized the Tanakh[46], as well as chastized their Jewish kinsmen to get them to do the same. Although they were the most devout of their day, Jesus set the bar higher.

> For I tell you, unless your righteousness surpasses that
> of the Pharisees and the teachers of the law, you will
> certainly not enter the kingdom of heaven – (Matthew
> 5: 20).

If religion won't work, then what will? Herein we have our answer: 'I am the way and the truth and the life. No one comes to the Father except through me' (John 14:6). The problem with the religious devotion of the Pharisees is that it was self-exalting. They prayed out of their energy. They gave out of their money. They memorized scripture to display their wisdom and lorded their hunger during fasts over a watching audience who would applaud their piety. Ultimately, Jesus is not calling us to be devoted to religion, but rather to be devoted to him. The word abide appears in 1 John many times; it's a key term to describe the attitude that we should take to the Christian life.

Jesus is the path of life; by abiding in him, we inevitably find our way to life. We do not follow him so that we gain financial, emotional or spiritual wealth; we are walking with Jesus, by the power of Jesus to get to Jesus. He is the one who empowers us. He is the one who forgives us when we fall. He is the means and the end. He is worth it, and walking with God is the most challenging and satisfying adventure on offer.

> I write these things to you who believe in the name of the Son of God so that you may know that you have eternal life – (1 John 5:13).

This is the point. John's gospel and his three letters have one obvious and overarching message: come to Jesus for there is nothing and no one better. John does not shy away from the hardships of believing in Jesus. Did you know that he wrote the book of Revelation having been banished to the isle of Patmos after being boiled alive (and surviving)? John also doesn't make the non-Christian life sound unsatisfying – he goes into detail about the allure of worldly things and the fleeting satisfaction they bring. However, John maintains that eternal life is better than wealth, orgasms, religion, fame, power or entertainment. God is the only water that will quench (remember the Samaritan woman in chapter 1?).

As we arrive at the closing chapter in John's book we see that he ends the way he started: by saying, 'You need Jesus'. I can join John and countless others in saying that Jesus has changed my entire life. There truly is nothing on this planet that gives me more purpose, love or fulfilment.

Exams. Qualifications. Job. Money. House. Car. Kids. Death. That's the mantra I've been told my entire life. Work hard to get good grades. Get good grades to get a good job. Get a good job to get lots of money. Get lots of money to get a nice house. Thereafter it's kind of up to you but cars, girls, kids and Prosecco are somewhere in the mix…then you die. That's it. Paint my face, put me in a box and let me return to the dust from whence I came.

It's jarring.

I just turned thirty-two and you're telling me that I'm halfway to thinking about retirement? My bones cry for more. You can't tell me I can sum up my entirety in four-score-and-seven. Or, if it's as simple as exams, jobs and death, maybe the end isn't soon enough? Life's either too short to enjoy or too long to bear. But that perspective completely misses the point.

God put the pull of eternity into my heart. He didn't make us for this glass ceiling, yet we all watch life slip like sand through our fingers. 'THERE'S MORE!' he screams from the cross. Didn't we hear him? Didn't we respond to his call from Calvary?

He made us for forever.

Our bodies that ache, bleed and creek will be restored to their proper glory. We were never meant to watch our days fade like autumn leaves but watch the tree blossom into a billion colours. I'm not home, yet. I'm not with dad, yet. But I hear him calling; every morning I'm a day closer. GCSEs aren't that important, salary is not paramount and the wooden box doesn't scare.

He made us for forever.

He made us to abide in him.

EPILOGUE: ABIDE IN THE SON

ACKNOWLEDGEMENTS

Firstly, to the only ballast that keeps my boat afloat, God you have been, continue to and will forever be the rock on which I build everything. You forgive the stumble and empower me to continue to pursue you. You are ultimate reality and without you, everything in this life tastes stale.

To my bride, this book has sparked several conversations between you and I, some difficult, some easy, but all helpful. I love you and cannot wait to start the adventure of a marriage together for the rest of my days.

To my inner circle, you actually are the best friends I could've ever asked for. Where on earth would I be if it wasn't for you?

To the Grace Church Youth, it was seven lovely years together. You're now fully grown adults walking through the madness that is 2020. I hope I did something of a half-decent job pointing you towards the Lord, forgive my ridiculousness. Ultimate Squidbee, anyone?

To the CrewMen, God bless you. This book was made for you. Thank you for being my inspiration to actually put pen to paper and help young people get closer to Jesus. I'm proud of the young men you've become. Thando Zulu, this book wouldn't have been a thing if it wasn't for you believing and enabling me to be part of your leadership team. Your foreword was the cherry on top of the cake.

To the Heart Church YA. I'm wrote this to hopefully put some steel in your spine and love in your heart after a very difficult year for the entire world.

To my advanced readers, your help was so pertinent at refining a very rough diamond.

Finally, to my editor Claire. Thank you for putting up with my complete naivety. Your patience, careful attention to every detail and theological insight crafted this book to something really beautiful.

ENDNOTES

PREFACE

1. Daniel Yudkin's 'More In Common' organization seeks to understand the forces that divide people, hoping for reconciliation. His paper 'The Perception Gap: How false impressions are pulling Americans apart' has been featured in CNN, the Financial Times, The Washington Post and more. They have found that the extremes of political discourse can make the US and UK feel polarized, whereas they only comprise 14 per cent of the electorate (progressive activists at 8 per cent and traditional conservatives at 6 per cent).

2. Luther M, Disputatio pro Declaratione Virtutis Indulgentiarum (Nuremberg: Hieronymus Höltzel; 1517).

3. G [pronounced gee] – shortened slang for 'gangsta'. Something everyone wants to be. If you know, you know.

COMMUNITY: ABIDE IN AUTHENTICITY

4. For those of you that've never heard the word 'evangelism', it means to preach a message to try and persuade people to believe this message. In Christianity, an evangelist would be anybody who goes around telling people about Jesus. But, as my point suggests, we are all evangelists – we tell everyone about stuff that we love.

BIBLE: ABIDE IN THE WORD

5. Barna Group, 'The State of The Bible Report' (New York: NY, 2014).

6. Naselli A., 'Three Tips for Better Bible reading', Desiring God website: https://www.desiringgod.org/articles/three-tips-for-better-Bible-reading, published 2014. Accessed 17 August 2018.

7. Feel inspired? Get involved at https://twloha.com

RHYTHM: ABIDE IN YOUR BODY

8. Smith J K. A., You Are What You Love: The Spiritual Power of Habit. (Ada, MI, Brazos Press, Division of Baker Publishing Group, 2016).

9. Breen M., Leading Kingdom Movements (Greenville, SC, 3DM, 2013).

10. The cow was also killed – sorry cow, you lived a purposeful existence.

11. The Campaign to End Loneliness, 'The Facts On Loneliness': https://www.campaigntoendloneliness.org/the-facts-on-loneliness/, published 2020. Accessed 22 August 2020.

12. Behr R., 'Alone Together: Why We Expect More from Technology and Less from Each Other by Sherry Turkle – review', The Guardian. Accessed 26 October 2020.

13. Samaritans. Suicide Statistics Report for the UK and ROI. Surrey; 2019. https://www.samaritans.org/documents/402/SamaritansSuicideStatsReport_2019_AcMhRyF.pdf. Accessed 13 Nov 2020

14. Heart Church Vision: https://heart.church/about, published 2018. Accessed August 22, 2020.

15. Office for National Statistics, 'Unemployment Rate (aged 16 and over, seasonally adjusted)': https://www.ons.gov.uk/employmentandlabourmarket/peoplenotinwork/unemployment/timeseries/mgsx/lms, Accessed 22 August 2020.

TRUTH: ABIDE IN DISCERNMENT

16. The Christian understanding of God is three-in-one: the Trinity. Although mathematically impossible, God is Father, Son and Holy Spirit.

17. Office for National Statistics, 'Overview of Violent Crime and Sexual Offences 2012/13' https://www.ons.gov.uk/peoplepopulationandcommunity/crimeandjustice/compendium/focusonviolentcrimeandsexualoffences/yearendingmarch2015/

chapter1overviewofviolentcrimeandsexualoffences, 2014. Accessed 22 August 2020.

18.   Anti-Bullying Alliance, 'Key Statistics': https://www. anti-bullyingalliance.org.uk/all-together-hub/audit-and-action-plan/1-school-leadership/15-we-monitor-pupil-absence-indication. Accessed 17 April 2019.

19.   Office for National Statistics, 'Statistical Bulletin Suicides in the United Kingdom, 2012 Registrations', 2013. https://www.ons.gov. uk/peoplepopulationandcommunity/birthsdeathsandmarriages/ deaths/bulletins/suicidesintheunitedkingdom/2014-02-18, Report Accessed 14 April 2016.

20.   United Nations, 'Universal Declaration of Human Rights', 1948, http://www.ohchr.org/EN/UDHR/Documents/ UDHR_Translations/eng.pdf, Accessed 18 April 2019.

FATHER: ABIDE IN DAD

21.   Luke is a fictious name and this story is an amalgam of many stories of many friends who have had difficult father stories. This chapter is about presenting the difficulty of believing in a perfect heavenly Father when you have a flawed (or absent) human father.

22.   Worringer S., 'Family Structure Still Matters': https:// www.centreforsocialjustice.org.uk/core/wp-content/ uploads/2020/08/CSJJ8372-Family-structure-Report-200807. pdf, published 2020. Accessed 25 August 2020.

23.   F. Broghammer, 'Cohabitation, Attachment, and Intergenerational Repetition' for Institute of Family Studies: https://ifstudies.org/ blog/cohabitation-attachment-and-intergenerational-repetition, published February 2020. Accessed 25 August 2020.

24.   Fatherhood Institute, 'Addressing Fatherlessness: How Government Can Strengthen the Active Presence of Fathers in Their Children's Lives', http://www.fatherhoodinstitute. org/2012/addressing-fatherlessness-a-fatherhood-institute-

policy-briefing/, published 2012. Accessed 25 August 2020.

25. Asthana A., 'Iain Duncan Smith Thinktank in "Fatherless Society" Warning': https://www.theguardian.com/lifeandstyle/2017/feb/12/fatherless-society-children-in-poverty-iain-duncan-smith--social-justice-thinktank, published February 2017. Accessed 27 September 2020.

26. Genesis 1 and 2, Psalm 8, Psalm 100 and Psalm 139 are chapters that emphasize the beauty and brilliance of the creation of humankind.

27. For the record, when I was a baby. I am yet to poo on my mother as an adult, but never say never.

28. Radford L., Corral S,. Bradley C., et al, Child Abuse and Neglect in the UK Today [Report] (London: National Society for the Prevention of Cruelty to Children, 2011).

WAR: DO NOT ABIDE IN SIN

29. Chopra D., Metahuman: Unleashing Your Infinite Potential (Rider, Danvers, MA, 2019).

30. The founding of the church at Thessalonica is recorded in Acts 17. This is one of the best examples of evangelism in the whole Bible. Because most of you are from the secular UK, this passage will help the Gospel make sense.

31. Mental Health Foundation. Boiling Point. London; 2008. https://www.mentalhealth.org.uk/sites/default/files/boilingpoint.pdf Accessed 24 August 2020

32. WebRoot, 'Internet Pornography by the Numbers; A Significant Threat to Society': https://www.webroot.com/us/en/resources/tips-articles/internet-pornography-by-the-numbers. Accessed 24 August 2020.

33. Watson J., The Homely Virtues (London: Hodder & Stoughton, 1903).

POWER: ABIDE IN THE SPIRIT

34.   Jones, Lora; Palumbo, Daniele; Brown D., 'Coronavirus: A visual guide to the economic impact', BBC Business: https://www.bbc.co.uk/news/business-51706225. Accessed 24 August 2020.

LOVE: ABIDE IN LOVE

35.   I have to admit, I was definitely more confused than sad because everybody knows there was enough space for both of them on that floating plank. Selfishness killed that relationship, not the cold.

36.   Adam and Eve's story can be found in Genesis 1–3.

37.   Abraham's story can be found in Genesis 11–18.

38.   There are 16 prophets in the Old Testament: Amos, Hosea, Jonah, Micah, Isaiah, Jeremiah, Obadiah, Habakkuk, Zephaniah, Joel, Nahum, Ezekiel, Daniel, Haggai, Zechariah & Malachi

39.   The book of Leviticus outlines the 5 types of offering that the Jewish people would have to ceremonially perform to restore the broken relationship between man and God: burnt offering, sin offering, guilt offering, grain offering & peace offering

40.   Leviticus 4:1 – 6:7 explains sin or guilt offerings

41.   Carson D.A., Scandalous (Illinois, InterVarsity Press, 2010.) I have to thank Don Carson for his wonderful exposition of Matthew 27. His chapter 'The ironies of the cross' explain this scene far better than I ever could.

FREEDOM: ABIDE IN PEACE

42.   The Northern Kingdom was conquered by Assyria in 722 BC (2 Kings 17). The Southern Kingdom was captured by Babylon in 605 BC (2 Kings 24:1–7).

43.   Cramer S. and Inkster B., 'Social Media and Young People's Mental Health and Wellbeing', Royal Society for Public Health: https://

www.rsph.org.uk/our-work/policy/social-media-and-young-people-s-mental-health-and-wellbeing.html. Accessed 26 October 2020.

44. Played by Benedict Cumberbatch in The Imitation Game, 2014.

EPILOGUE: ABIDE IN THE SON

45. Welsh for 'red-ridge'.

46. The thirty-nine books of the Old Testament, totalling roughly
     800,000 words. To put it into context, the entire Lord of
     the Rings series (including The Hobbit) has 576,459.

APPENDIX ONE: ANSWERS TO BIBLE QUIZ

1. Who wrote the first five books of the Old Testament?
   Moses.

2. Why did God rescue his people from slavery under Pharaoh in Egypt?
   To take them to the promised land (modern-day Israel/Palestine). It would be a place where they could love God freely without fear of slavery.

3. Who was king of Israel before David?
   Saul – the first king of Israel.

4. If the Northern Kingdom was called Israel, what was the Southern Kingdom called?
   Judah.

5. Why did God send prophets to his people in the Old Testament?
   God's prophets in the Old Testament were sent to speak on behalf of God. They would often take words of encouragement, correction and/or judgement, all in the hope of restoring God's people back to their glorious selves.

6. Who told everyone that Jesus was coming?
   John the Baptist preached that the Kingdom of Heaven was near, and that Jesus was the one Isaiah had prophesied about (see Matthew 3).

7. What did Jesus tell all Christians to do before ascending
    to heaven?
    *'Make disciples of all nations, baptizing them in
    the name of the Father and of the Son and of the
    Holy Spirit, and teaching them to obey everything I
    have commanded you' (Matthew 28:19–20). This is
    known as the Great Commission.*

8. What happened when Peter the Apostle preached for the
    first time in Jerusalem?
    *The Holy Spirit fell like tongues of fire on the gathered
    assembly in Jerusalem and 3,000 people were added
    to the church that day. This is known as Pentecost
    (Acts 2).*

9. What was Paul / Saul of Tarsus doing before he became a
    Christian?
    *Saul of Tarsus was a fierce persecutor of Christians,
    dragging them from their homes to prison for their
    new-found faith in Jesus. Acts 9 describes his dramatic
    conversion to Christianity.*

10. What book of the Bible describes the end of the world?
    *Revelation. That book was also written by John the
    Apostle (in addition to the gospel of John and 1–3
    John).*

APPENDIX TWO: BIBLE READING PLANS

2A: THE JESUS READING PLAN

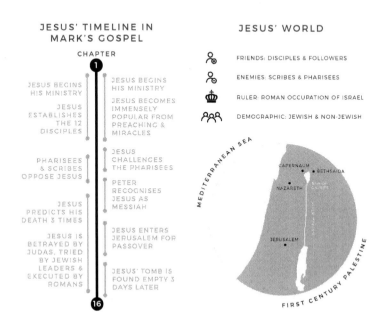

JESUS' TIMELINE IN MARK'S GOSPEL

CHAPTER
1

JESUS BEGINS HIS MINISTRY

JESUS ESTABLISHES THE 12 DISCIPLES

JESUS BEGINS HIS MINISTRY

JESUS BECOMES IMMENSELY POPULAR FROM PREACHING & MIRACLES

PHARISEES & SCRIBES OPPOSE JESUS

JESUS CHALLENGES THE PHARISEES

PETER RECOGNISES JESUS AS MESSIAH

JESUS PREDICTS HIS DEATH 3 TIMES

JESUS IS BETRAYED BY JUDAS, TRIED BY JEWISH LEADERS & EXECUTED BY ROMANS

JESUS ENTERS JERUSALEM FOR PASSOVER

JESUS' TOMB IS FOUND EMPTY 3 DAYS LATER

16

JESUS' WORLD

FRIENDS: DISCIPLES & FOLLOWERS

ENEMIES: SCRIBES & PHARISEES

RULER: ROMAN OCCUPATION OF ISRAEL

DEMOGRAPHIC: JEWISH & NON-JEWISH

MEDITERRANEAN SEA

CAPERNAUM ● ● BETHSAIDA

NAZARETH ●

JERUSALEM ●

FIRST CENTURY PALESTINE

BREAKDOWN OF THE FOUR GOSPELS

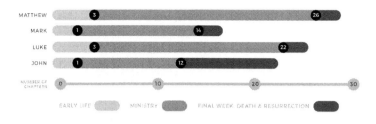

MATTHEW — 3 — 26

MARK — 1 — 14

LUKE — 3 — 22

JOHN — 1 — 12

NUMBER OF CHAPTERS: 0 — 10 — 20 — 30

EARLY LIFE | MINISTRY | FINAL WEEK: DEATH & RESURRECTION

QUESTIONS

1. WHERE WAS JESUS?
2. WHAT WAS JESUS DOING?
3. WHY WAS JESUS DOING THIS?
4. WHO DID JESUS THINK HE WAS?

2B: THE JEWISH CHURCH READING PLAN

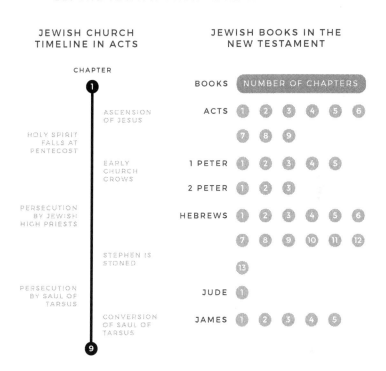

JEWISH CHURCH TIMELINE IN ACTS

CHAPTER

1

ASCENSION OF JESUS

HOLY SPIRIT FALLS AT PENTECOST

EARLY CHURCH GROWS

PERSECUTION BY JEWISH HIGH PRIESTS

STEPHEN IS STONED

PERSECUTION BY SAUL OF TARSUS

CONVERSION OF SAUL OF TARSUS

9

JEWISH BOOKS IN THE NEW TESTAMENT

BOOKS — NUMBER OF CHAPTERS

ACTS 1 2 3 4 5 6
7 8 9

1 PETER 1 2 3 4 5

2 PETER 1 2 3

HEBREWS 1 2 3 4 5 6
7 8 9 10 11 12
13

JUDE 1

JAMES 1 2 3 4 5

BREAKDOWN OF ACTS

CHAPTER IN ACTS

1 — 9 — 16 — 28

JEWISH CHURCH — TRANSITION — UNIVERSAL CHURCH

QUESTIONS

1. WHAT WAS THE HOLY SPIRIT DOING?
2. WHAT WERE THE DISCIPLES DOING?
3. WHO LOVED THE CHURCH? WHY?
4. WHO HATED THE CHURCH? WHY?

APPENDIX TWO: BIBLE READING PLANS
2C: THE CHURCH IN TRANSITION READING PLAN

**THE TRANSITION OF
THE CHURCH IN ACTS**

**BOOKS WRITTEN IN
THE TRANSITION**

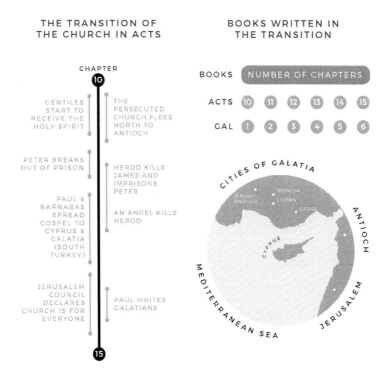

CHAPTER
10

GENTILES
START TO
RECEIVE THE
HOLY SPIRIT

THE
PERSECUTED
CHURCH FLEES
NORTH TO
ANTIOCH

PETER BREAKS
OUT OF PRISON

HEROD KILLS
JAMES AND
IMPRISONS
PETER

PAUL &
BARNABAS
SPREAD
GOSPEL TO
CYPRUS &
GALATIA
(SOUTH
TURKEY)

AN ANGEL KILLS
HEROD

JERUSALEM
COUNCIL
DECLARES
CHURCH IS FOR
EVERYONE

PAUL WRITES
GALATIANS

15

BOOKS NUMBER OF CHAPTERS

ACTS 10 11 12 13 14 15

GAL 1 2 3 4 5 6

CITIES OF GALATIA

PISIDIAN ANTIOCH   ICONIUM   LYSTRA   DERBE

CYPRUS

ANTIOCH

MEDITERRANEAN SEA

JERUSALEM

BREAKDOWN OF ACTS

CHAPTER IN ACTS

1   9   16   28

JEWISH
CHURCH

TRANSITION

UNIVERSAL
CHURCH

QUESTIONS

1. WHAT WAS THE HOLY SPIRIT DOING?
2. WHAT WERE THE DISCIPLES DOING?
3. WHERE WAS THE GOSPEL GOING?
4. WHO HATED THE CHURCH? WHY?

2D: THE UNIVERSAL CHURCH READING PLAN

THE UNIVERSAL CHURCH IN ACTS

BOOKS FOR JEWS & GENTILES IN THE NEW TESTAMENT

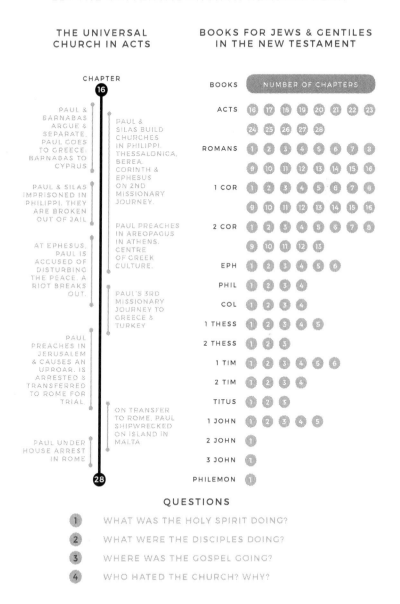

CHAPTER
16

PAUL & BARNABAS ARGUE & SEPARATE. PAUL GOES TO GREECE. BARNABAS TO CYPRUS

PAUL & SILAS BUILD CHURCHES IN PHILIPPI, THESSALONICA, BEREA, CORINTH & EPHESUS ON 2ND MISSIONARY JOURNEY.

PAUL & SILAS IMPRISONED IN PHILIPPI. THEY ARE BROKEN OUT OF JAIL

PAUL PREACHES IN AREOPAGUS IN ATHENS. CENTRE OF GREEK CULTURE.

AT EPHESUS, PAUL IS ACCUSED OF DISTURBING THE PEACE. A RIOT BREAKS OUT.

PAUL'S 3RD MISSIONARY JOURNEY TO GREECE & TURKEY

PAUL PREACHES IN JERUSALEM & CAUSES AN UPROAR. IS ARRESTED & TRANSFERRED TO ROME FOR TRIAL

ON TRANSFER TO ROME, PAUL SHIPWRECKED ON ISLAND IN MALTA

PAUL UNDER HOUSE ARREST IN ROME

28

BOOKS	NUMBER OF CHAPTERS							
ACTS	16	17	18	19	20	21	22	23
	24	25	26	27	28			
ROMANS	1	2	3	4	5	6	7	8
	9	10	11	12	13	14	15	16
1 COR	1	2	3	4	5	6	7	8
	9	10	11	12	13	14	15	16
2 COR	1	2	3	4	5	6	7	8
	9	10	11	12	13			
EPH	1	2	3	4	5	6		
PHIL	1	2	3	4				
COL	1	2	3	4				
1 THESS	1	2	3	4	5			
2 THESS	1	2	3					
1 TIM	1	2	3	4	5	6		
2 TIM	1	2	3	4				
TITUS	1	2	3					
1 JOHN	1	2	3	4	5			
2 JOHN	1							
3 JOHN	1							
PHILEMON	1							

QUESTIONS

1. WHAT WAS THE HOLY SPIRIT DOING?
2. WHAT WERE THE DISCIPLES DOING?
3. WHERE WAS THE GOSPEL GOING?
4. WHO HATED THE CHURCH? WHY?

ΛGONIZƆ

IF YOU LIKED THIS BOOK, YOU MAY LIKE THIS

Do you value your faith, but struggle to
put it into everyday practice? Agonizo is for
you. Agonizo is Greek for 'struggle'. Our
mission is simple: link God's word to your
world. With freebies, the weekly newsletter
and so much more, come check us out.

Sign up today and get a Free E-book:
Beginner's Guide to the New Testament.
Follow the link or Scan the QR Code

struggl.life/join

Printed in Great Britain
by Amazon

59544840R00097